DEAR DIRTY DUBLIN

DEAR DIRTY DUBLIN

a discursion . . . or something

G. W. Target

illustrations by
John Holdcroft

1974
GALLIARD
LONDON
STAINER & BELL LTD

SBN 85249 296 0

Printed in Great Britain by Galliard (Printers) Ltd Great Yarmouth

To the Memory of my Grandmother

MOORE STREET MARKET.
DUBLIN.

"Dublin," it says here, "is the Capital City of the Irish Republic."
Well now, you can't be saying fairer than *that*, now *can* you?

"It lies," it says, so it does, obviously with lost Aer Lingus pilots circling above the lingering mists of the Celtic Twilight like the Seven Wild Geese of Carrigahooley Castle, "in latitude 53° 20′ 38″ north of the equator, and in longitude 6° 17′ 30″ west of Greenwich."

And, like your actual Dubliner, I'll fight any bloody man to deny it.

"It'd be a poor bloody man who wouldn't, so he would. But then, did you ever hear tell of the. . . ."

Which is to carry on before we've a drink taken, surely?

"I've never heard a truer thing said! And I'll not be the one to be refusing a pint of plain porter in me fist as a mark of this occasion!"

And should I then presume?
And how should I begin?

"Begin at the beginning," said the King to the White Rabbit, very gravely, "and go on till you come to the end: then stop."

"You'd not be quoting a book the like of that to be starting a few words on the Capital City of the Republic?"

Sorry, mavourin, me ould darlin' man, but there are few books more to the present point than *Alice's Adventures in Wonderland*. . . .

Unless, that is, you'd prefer a few words of blarney lapped in a tide of peat-coloured Guinness?

> "Dear Erin, how sweetly thy green bosom rises!
> An emerald set in the ring of the sea.
> Each blade of thy meadows my faithful heart prizes,
> Thou Queen of the West, the world's Cushla-ma-Chree."

Though, being that sort of a country, there *are* other opinions. . . .

"Ireland," says the Ginger Man himself, "shrunken teat on the chest of the cold Atlantic."

"The old sow that eats her farrow," says Stephen Dedalus. . . .

"I have never seen farrow eaten by a sow in my life," says Seamus Heaney, and him brought up on an Irish farm. "What *would* happen is that the young pigs eat one another's ears."

Well, yes, come to think of it, that'll do just as fine!

> *Out of Ireland have we come:*
> *Great hatred, little room,*
> *Maimed us from the start. . . .*

By day or night it's incredible, larger than life and less than the truth, extravagant, mean, broad and narrow, one foot in the gutter and both eyes cocked at the wheeling stars, exuberant, given to the delights of despair, all things to some men, some things to a few, nothing to fewer, the sun and the moon to the completely besotted, prodigious, depressing, astonishing, unutterable. . . .

And then the Thesaurus peters out in synonyms.

O John McCormack (1884–1945) where is thy music?

Kodak! where, O where are thy ultra-fast colour-reversal Kodachrome films perfect for glowing transparencies?

O *Reader's Digest!* what would it pay me to Improve my Word Power?

Might be safer to stick with what it *almost* says here:

"The word 'Dublin' is an English form of *Dubh-Linn* ('Dark Pool'), the name given by the Native Irish of ancient days to the Guinness-coloured estuary waters of the River Liffey."

Guinness-coloured?

The last time I had the heart in me to stand on the O'Connell

Bridge and look down at the "hitherandthithering waters" of the Liffey. . . .

(Thank *you*, James Joyce.)

. . . they were a dirty sort of dark indeterminate green, with a scum of yellow suds congealing along the slime of Eden Quay, and a smear of iridescent oil-slick on its sluggish way to kiss the, er, "white breast of the dim sea." And a drowning newspaper wrapped against the wet curve of stone below. And all manner of soggy fagends and sinking cartons and bits of broken wood and bobbing shapes of irreducible plastic. And this dead tabby-cat drifting on its back with this fat white belly to it.

'Twas not, as they do say, always thus. . . .

"The seat of this citie," wrote Stainihurst I don't know how long ago, "is of all sides pleasant, comfortable and wholesome. If you would traverse hills, they are not far off. If champaign ground, it lieth of all parts. If you be delited with fresh water, the famous river called the Liffie runneth fast by. If you will take the view of the sea, it is at hand. . . ."

With some of that Great Golden Legend remaining to be seen if you don't look too closely, or keep your Dark Rosaleen sun-glasses on at all times of the enfabled day and dreaming night, or only go where your Package Tour is Conducted, or refrain from asking too many awkward questions of quite the wrong people. . . .

In short, if you'll not be making a bloody nuisance of yourself rocking the bloody boat.

True, in the purple prose of the nearest Guide Book, "a salt wind blows into the teeming heart of the Seventh City of Christendom, and the gentle outlines and friendly slopes of the Wicklow Hills seem to rise and draw our willing eyes with their enchantment at the end of every street in the southern suburbs" . . . but the heart suffers from fatty degeneration of its sentimental tissues, and those streets are blocked off from more than the Hills of Wicklow by mountains of mouldering nostalgia.

Though you know what Guide Books are.

9

For as the Blessed Saint Patrick himself set his holy foot on the sombre beauty of Number One platform at Ameins Street Station. . . .

"Wouldn't you be knowing they've changed its name since his day?"

. . . having come down from Belfast *via* the. . . .

"Though it's more than names they've been changing—for couldn't you once be seeing Nelson up on his column from the steps of this same station? And a fine job you'd have to be seeing it now, surely!"

(Patience, friend—that's the secret. And just don't lose the thread —for here's a labyrinth built by the old father, the old artificer himself.

Look *that* up in your Greek Myths!)

Wasn't there something about a Guide Book?

Well, you know the way *they* wander. . . .

As the Blessed Saint Patrick himself set his holy foot on the sombre beauty of Number One platform at the railway station (whatever it's called these changing days), having come down from Belfast *via* the. . . .

"Now wouldn't that be the troubled city, surely?"

. . . having come down from the admittedly troubled city of. . . .

"With it being the Protestants making the trouble!"

Is it the Protestants planting bombs to be killing women and children?

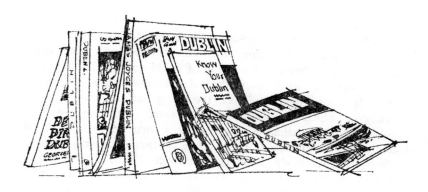

"They've done their share of murdering good Catholics!"
Does murdering Protestants bring dead Catholics to life?
"Would you be having us knuckle under to black tyranny?"
You expect *them* to knuckle under to a Green one!
"And why not? With green the only colour for the flag of Ireland!"
(Let it go. What's the use fighting a man for the colour of his flag?)
Er . . . having come down from, er . . . Well, having come *via* the
fast service of trains over a network connecting many major centres,
he was handed an Official Guide Book as issued by the Authority
vested in the Corporation of the City of Dublin—or, to call the City
by its restored Irish name, *Baile Atha Cliath* ('The Ford of the
Hurdles'), thus reminding us of the famous bridge of wattle-hurdles
and green boughs made by Conor MacNessa, a Northern Chieftain,
who was returning home from a raid on the King of Leinster, and
found his retreat hindered by an unexpected flooding of the Liffey,
so it was.

Mind you, to be putting the matter straight. . . .
"Wouldn't it be a poor bloody man to be leaving it the way it was?"
. . . the Blessed Saint Patrick got precious little change from the new
pound-note he tendered, as he was obviously a Tourist and a tyro
with the currency, but, in gratitude. . . .
"Well, wasn't himself the grateful man?"
. . . but, in gratitude, he converted many of the inhabitants to
Roman Catholicism. . . .

"Glory be to God!"

... which gave a most decided fillip to the Religious Life of the whole community, a tradition which has persisted until recent date, and also caused a miraculous spring of world-renowned soda-water to gush forth in either his Cathedral towering above its humble surroundings on Nicholas Street, the flying buttresses and Choral Services of which are deservedly celebrated, with the powerful personality of Jonathan Swift, the most virulent Satirist in all Literature, best known as the Author of that children's Classic, *Gulliver's Travels*, having been its Dean from 1713 to 1745, and who now lies entombed where, in the words of his own bitter and immortal epitaph, "Furious Indignation Can No Longer Rend His Heart," or at the end of Nassau Street. . . .

"Now why would himself want his spring on Nassau Street? Will you be telling me that though I sit here the long Sundays of Lent?"

... which leads out onto Grafton Street, Dublin's most fashionable thoroughfare of exclusive shops, a Mecca for discriminating shoppers. . . .

"Mother of God! they'd charge you the bloody earth for sunshine!"

... where, within the mellowed walls of Number 17, Percy Bysshe Shelley stayed with his young wife on their visit in 1812. They had many notable callers, among them Curran, who came twice to dinner, and at several other times. The couple were strict vegetarians, though it was from a house on the site of Number 7 that the Poet distributed his stirring *Address to the Irish People* in the year of 1818.

But, whichever spring be the true one. . . .

"It was never on Nassau Street though I sit here the murdering Sundays of the next nine Lents!"

... but, whichever, it possesses many healing and medicinal qualities to which multitudes have testified. . . .

"Though, with himself the one to forgive me, it's no bloody match for a gill of your water from the Grotto of Lourdes!"

... and it is occasionally used to. . . .

"I mean, did you ever hear tell of the woman of Glengarriff in the County of Cork, her with the incurable growth to her body? She made the Three Novenas of Supplication to Our Blessed Lady of Lourdes,

12

OUR LADY OF DUBLIN. — HANDCRAFT? —

took a sup of the water on an empty stomach before reciting the Five Decades of the Rosary for that morning, with the water brought home from a Pilgrimage the previous Easter by her married sister, a woman of Skibbereen—and wasn't she cured completely? with never a trace left? Which was told me by my mother's own cousin in Macroom, who knows them both, so he does."

But, whichever be the true spring of the Blessed Saint Patrick. . . .

"With it never on Nassau Street!"

. . . its product is occasionally used to adulterate Irish whiskey. . . .

"A most distressful custom, surely now!"

13

... as may be witnessed by an Evening Jaunt around Dublin's Singing Pubs, Advance Booking Advisable to Avoid Disappointment, though the metropolis, with its aqueduct of 22-miles from the Wicklow Mountains, constructed by Sir John Grey in 1868, has a water-supply remarkable for its purity—not to mention some of the finest examples of both Public and Domestic Architecture extant in the whole of Europe, mostly Georgian, around which, after countless vicissitudes, High Romance clings in a fretted palimpsest on which the most vivid characters and exciting events of both Ancient and Modern History have inscribed their turbulent legend, impressing innumerable visitors from the wide world over with a galaxy of brilliant contributions to the culture and enlightenment of Mankind thus quickening the imagination to a kinship with Ireland's rich heritage.

"By Jesus!" says he, "I never heard the like of it in all my born puff!"

And there you have it, in the words of himself there, the one with

14

the fresh pint of plain porter to his fist: the codding, the blarney, the wheedling to the voice, the ceaseless blathering, the mockery with an edge so feathering gentle you don't always feel it razoring to the bone, the drink taken, the passing of the time of day. . . .

Paddy as the Uncle Tom of Europe.

"I described Ireland," wrote Yeats, "as a little greasy huckstering nation groping for halfpence in a greasy till, but did not add, except in thought, *by the light of a holy candle.*"

"Mother of God!" says himself, "if you're not liking the bloody place, you know where the bloody boat leaves from!"

Well, if you don't know it now you never bloody will!

"The most popular Irish entertainment," says Sean O'Faolain (pronounced *Shawn O'Forlorn* by them as don't know their Erse from their elbow), a man from the City of Cork who has the sort of name to him which sounds as though he'd be the sort to be knowing the like of this, surely, "is to circumspect, and to disagree."

So, if you want to get from here to there, straight, bang, in and out, no blathering nonsense, *and* come back the same person you were before you paid your Off-Peak Bargain-Rate Inclusive Fare. . . .

Well, sorry, but you're on the wrong Conducted Tour altogether —for, on *this* little caper, the "longest way round is the shortest way home, and the means more important than the end."

(Thank *you*, George Moore.)

And if you want to view the Artistic Glories, the Stately Architecture and Magnificent Vistas, the Ornamental Ceilings and Majestic Interiors, and all such reminders of other days around us, you'll just have to request kind permission of the, er, appropriate Management: *Special Prices Upon Personal Application.*

Though a few silver coins of the Realm in the palm of the discreet hand would be opening many another door, surely.

A nod as good as a wink to those with a mind for such things

"From this time on," says Françoise Henry, who has published many studies in Irish Art, so she has, "new motifs appear in great number, side by side with the curvilinear theme, but," says she, "it is this complex and sinuous system of linear combinations which is to remain the framework and the norm . . . which," says she, "is an art with a taste for bewildering the beholder by its unexpected and hidden rhythms."

Which, again, is another thing you can't be saying fairer than *that*, now *can* you?

As for disagreeing. . . .

Wait now!

For are we not a people given to disagreement?

Have we not murdered one another about which end of the egg of Ireland to be eating our breakfast from? Which colour of a bloody flag to be slaughtering women and children for?

"So soon as the bloody man overtook me half-way along bloody Talbot Street, wasn't he but a bloody word and a quicker bloody fist?"

And who's bloody fool enough to be wanting a quick fist in the bloody gob half-way along any bloody street?

So: *It is becoming now to declare my allegiance* . . . and thus give you the chance to discount my prejudices.

I have lived in Dublin all the days of my life. . . .

> *For 'tis the Capital of the finest Nation,*
> *Wid charmin' peasantry on a fruitful sod,*
> *Fightin' like Divils for conciliation,*
> *An' hatin' each other for the Love of God!*

True, it's been called London, Florence, New York, Hastings, or Fort Collins, Colorado—but I have never really left the streets I scuffed my boots on as a boy with Martin Mooney and Michael Kinsella. . . .

Strange how the names suddenly present themselves. . . .

Haven't thought about them all these years. . . .

That wart Martin Mooney had on the thumb of his hand. . . .

"What *that's* wanting," said a boy in Miss Flynn's class, "is dipping three times in the stone trough where a mare has drunk the twice in the one day."

And we watched most of one August afternoon by a tank for the prancing creatures out at Ballsbridge during the Royal Dublin Society Horse Show, with us not knowing the difference between a mare and a gelding, and Martin Mooney dipping in his hand three times after every horse to be making sure, the good smell of the creatures on us, and their droppings still caked on the soles of our boots when we got back home. . . .

But the wart never shifted for man nor beast.

"Was it a *stone* trough?" said the boy in Miss Flynn's class. . . .

Or the way Michael Kinsella would dander. . . .

Dander?

Well, isn't that the walk of a man? The way you'd be knowing him when he's too far down the street to tell by the cast of his eye or the cut of his hair, surely?

Well, Michael Kinsella's dander had this spring to it, and you'd know him by the bounce of his head and the lift of his heels. . . .

Or what you had to say and do in certain ritual circumstances. . . .

"Aren't you the big liar!" would say someone. . . .

And you'd have to say *Here's my own Holy Missal*, and hold your hands pressed together like the pages of a closed book and then open them out . . . *Here's my gob and loudest whistle*, and spit a gob in the gutter and let go a whistle as loud as the Last Trumpet of Judgement . . . *And here's my right hand up to Heaven*, and lift up your hand and point with your first finger and risk all the wrath of Almighty God if it *was* a lie you'd been telling to the danger of your immortal soul.

And, after *that*, you'd be obliged to fight anyone who went on calling you the big liar—or, worse, *be* both a liar *and* a whinging coward.

Whinging?

Well, isn't that crying when you'd no cause to be crying?

Or what you had to do in *other* ritual circumstances. . . .

17

To INCENSE anything or anyone take the top of the chains of the THURIBLE in the left hand and place it against the breast. Take the chains close above the shut cover in the right. It is important not to hold the chains far from the cover, or the thurible may swing out too far and will perhaps get entangled in the chains. . . .

Which happened to me at Benediction the very first time Father Lynch trusted me with it, and hadn't he taught me with his own hands?

There are two ways of incensing: with a SIMPLE SWING (ductus simplex) and with a DOUBLE SWING (ductus duplex). The simple swing is made in this way: lift the right hand to the. . . .

(And what was the name of that girl from the far end of Holles Street? Fight any one of us as soon as we'd look sideways at her. Scratch, bite, scream, kick, bring up a knee where girls weren't supposed to bloody know about—*and* swear worse than any man we'd ever heard.)

With them, and all the others, all the remembered faces and forgotten names, I was brought up and educated as a Roman Catholic, and the Sundays and Holy Days of my youth were enraptured with all the glory and beauty of Liturgy and Ceremonial: High Mass sung in Latin, the Priest robed in satin and cloth of gold, the voices of us boys rising sweet and clear in praise of Almighty God and Jesus Christ and the Blessed Virgin Mary . . . all that incense, the ascensions of candles, the lamps and votive lights, the blaze of Benediction, the tinkling bells, the Litanies, the Names and Invocations of all those Blessed Saints. . . .

(Teresa Riordan, that was the name of that girl. . . . Gave me her Sacred Heart Medal for my Rosary when I was entered for a Seminary.)

For various reasons, mostly personal and largely irrelevant, I am now a Protestant—but will allow no mere Priest to rob me of my birthright, no mere Denomination to arrogate the Voice of God unto itself alone. In other words I remain a Catholic in what I hope

18

is the best and widest sense, and still get more blessing out of Monteverdi's *Vespro della Beata Vergine* of 1610 than all the sermons Billy Graham ever preached.

(Wonder whatever became of Martin Mooney and Michael Kinsella?)

Apart from the Songs and the Literature which arose from its bitter ashes, and a natural sympathy both for the victims of oppression and those who rebel against it (though not always for what they *do*), I have little interest in the murderous politics of Ireland, such constricting and mean-minded nationalism being one of the deadlier diseases of the body politic. *That* sort of "love" for your country almost invariably implies hatred of *other* countries. True, we can love the sights and sounds and smells of our countryside, enjoy the company of our fellow-countrymen, relish the lilt and cadence of our language, and be rightly proud of our truly human contribution to the rest of humanity: Art, Science, Literature, Music . . . magnanimity, humour, compassion, charity . . . but the "patriotic" history of almost any country is shameful and degrading, merely a tendentious account of the squalid doings of Kings and "Great Men" who have marched in blood across the face of Man.

And "all *our* histories," says Sean O'Faolain, "are nationalist, patriotic, political, sentimental."

And Dublin, of *all* cities, is no place of recent beginnings and happy endings, of short memories and fresh starts—but, rather, of the dreams we *call* History, the promises we postpone till Tomorrow, the confusion we confuse with Reality, the stones we accept for Living Bread. . . .

High Rhetoric? Gone flat through being the last drainings of an exhausted well that was always tainted, always suspect?

Agreed—but that's what it does to you: maims even language.

So a stupid brawl becomes a Battle Fought for a Shimmering Vision, a professional politician juggling with putrefying ideas is the Saviour of His People, and men kill and die for the words of a sentimental song.

"Jesus," says he in Barney Kiernan's pub, "there's always some bloody clown or other kicking up a bloody murder about bloody nothing. Gob, it'd turn the porter sour in your guts, so it would."

Another nod as good as a wink from Françoise Henry

"It is a mental game," says she, who has been attached to the National University of Ireland, so she has, "which delights in meanders, in disconcerting equivalences of form and colour. . . . Spirals and interlacings," says she, "a network of fine threads . . . in red, green and yellow . . . bright blue," says she, "a scintillating tracery of gold filigree, separated by raised bands of amber, studs of coloured enamel and carved amber held in place by fine filigreed beading."

Such high comparisons are, of course, the sweetest form of self-flattery and ego-tripping, but, er . . . well, if you don't sound your own trumpet you have to pay a bloody trumpeter—and you know how expensive *they* can be these days, don't you?

So, for a few last top notes, thank *you*, Miss Henry!

"It is based," says she, who has made it her special study, so she has, "on a refusal of reality . . . sometimes pure dialectics," says she, "an intellectual exercise which owes nothing to the outside world . . . a dream of a pliant and malleable universe," says she, "at once subtle, coherent and harmonious in its strangeness . . . labyrinthine," says she, "this disciplined effervescence of the imagination. . . ."

Put it any plainer, and we'd risk submerging in a knee-deep wash of learned footnotes, and then being dragged under by the upper and lower mill-stones of *References* and *Select Bibliography*.

Me and the Book of bloody Kells!

★   ★   ★

So there, then, as treacherous and ungrateful as you need to believe for the defence and gratification of your own beliefs, my allegiance . . . and there, for as far as your own can discount in charity or sorrow, my snivelling prejudices.

The rest, between ourselves and the mattress on Molly Bloom's bed, is as much Dublin as we can make it.

Which is presumption enough, *and* to be sparing, for any man!

★   ★   ★

A Reminder of the Reality behind the Blather
The day after the latest explosion in Belfast . . .
IRA BOMB INJURES 34
. . . I was on the Morning Express down to that Number One platform, and the man opposite me saw that I was interested in the headlines of his paper.

"More likely to have been the Protestant Vanguard Movement," he said to me, but loud enough for the compartment. "Which wouldn't be the first time they've tried to shift the blame. Keep the pot boiling, that's their scheme. Twist the knife in the green wound."

I was naturally embarrassed at being caught having a free read, and so I muttered something about having to run for the train and not getting a chance to buy a. . . .

21

O' CONNELL MONUMENT. DUBLIN. Hardcraft

22

"They've done it many a time before," he said. "Murdered their own and made it look to be the work of Republicans. Destroyed power-stations and left Sinn Fein literature. Haven't they been doing the like these many years?"

There was little I could have said which would have been much good against the clatter of the wheels and the cast of his mind, and, *these* days, on *that* subject, a quiet tongue turneth away a lot of grief . . . so I did my best to slide out from under the lunacy of our history by making some non-committal noises . . . and your man seemed disappointed.

"The old game," he said, "blackening the reputation of Patriots. Look what they did to Parnell. Which is not to say there hasn't been faults on both sides. What man in his right mind would deny that there's been the mistakes made? But the shooting of soldiers is one thing, for what right have they in this country at all? Have we no obligation to be defending our own soil? And the destruction of property—if it drives out the Bankers, the Industrialists of a Foreign Power occupying us by the gun, with the blood on the streets of Derry to prove it. . . . Well, who doesn't want to see the backs of the exploiters of any country? But when there's loss of life in the destruction, when there's civilians injured, as in this explosion yesterday—well, it's the Protestants keeping the pot boiling, for we have no quarrel with the innocent, and give fair warning before, the phone message for the police to be clearing the area. Which, being Protestant police, they don't always do as quickly as they could. For what's a few more lives to the likes of them, will you tell me that? When it's Republicans to be landed with the blame? I tell you, there's nothing they wouldn't stoop to!"

But, eventually, he must have seen that I wasn't the right person for that sort of soft-soap and soap-box, and he spent the rest of the journey down through all those miles of lovely country. . . .

Dundalk, Dromiskin, Dunleer, Drogheda, Balbriggan, Malahide . . . the Holy Land of Ireland to our right, the sea so often glimpsed to our left, the Six Counties behind us in their misery, Dublin our destination. . . .

23

. . . reading the rest of his paper and glancing at the slender legs of the Swedish girl sitting in the far corner.

And, once past Raheny and Killester and Fairview Park, once out at the station, he gathered his things and ditched his paper and walked down the length of Number One platform a few steps this side of her, not missing a thing, not a toss of the long blonde hair, not a movement of flesh beneath her loose white dress—and she was beautiful, clean and cool, young and alive all over . . . vulnerable. . . .

And I saw her lying on a street in Belfast, the bright blood gouting, the bones splintering, pain bubbling in her throat. . . .

And there was your man giving his ticket to the collector at the barrier, and going on down the steps into the world we have made . . . into Dublin and along the pavements of his personal Hell.

Now even James Joyce himself didn't think that "any writer has yet presented Dublin to the world."

And who else dare try since Finnegan slept?

Hasn't himself told *all* the Tales of Shem and Shaun?

And who *are* the living sons or daughters of Anna Livia Plurabelle? *(Postcards only, please!)*

Yet, come to think of it, "every attempt is a wholly new start" (if only a "different kind of failure" at the finish) . . . and, again, all even James Joyce himself started to produce was a "chapter in the moral history of (our) country."

Some chapter!

However, on *those* terms there might still perhaps be a littering of footnotes to stand the weight of a few paragraphs, a cluster of small epiphanies still to be experienced. . . .

Was talking to this middle-aged man in the Autumn sun of

St Stephen's Green when a couple of young American girls walked on
by towards Grafton Street with their Guide Books.

Walked?

They were in tight blue jeans, worn pale and thin by use or bleached
to order, cut short above the knee and carefully frayed, ragged for an
extra few dollars, with a large heart-shaped patch to each resilient
left buttock (one yellow, one scarlet), riding on what they knew they
had, knowing what they were doing with it (having seen an old
movie of Marilyn Monroe) and yet not fully aware of what it did,
moving to bounce, to shake that thing (having heard some old Jazz
on record), flaunting their new breasts beneath their white shirts,
yet strangely innocent in their corrupted Eden, alive all the way up,
naked all over under whatever else they had on, wanton, wilful, and
yet still only going through the surface motions of deliberate inten-
tion . . . but, call it what you fancy, it was never a walk: a shimmy
like everybody's young sister Kate . . . all the highly-charged images

of lust or yearning summoned from what troubled depths . . . time past and lost youth. . . .

But it was never a *walk*.

"Holy Mother of God," says this man, pretending to groan with comical desire, trying to make it sound casual, and nearly succeeding, "who'd be a Priest in this bloody Holy City?"

An epiphany: not necessarily a "showing forth of Christ" in the old theological sense (though it was also that, after its own fashion), but a sudden manifestation of essentials, a telling like it is, a moment of eternity in which the world is seen in a heart-shaped patch, heard in a groan of desire for the unattainable, regret for the way it used to be, some other place, some other time. . . .

First Colour-slide from a Set of Six—Obtainable at all Gift Shops

SANDYCOVE: The dark blue-green of the Irish Sea, the Hill of Howth merging with the scudding slate-grey clouds on the sweeping rim of the horizon's pencilled line, tides of ultramarine, currents of almost purple, the slowly heaving ground-swell of nearly indigo, wave-tops of silver catching the last of the westering light far out from the purling shore, ripples curling and slapping, lapping the tumbled rocks, smooth and slimed, swirling with weed and tangles of net, gear, broken wood, dead fish torn at by crabs, scavengers, stones, crushed shells, the water cold, translucent . . . with the pale glistening flesh of a man at the Forty-foot Bathing Place, his genitals pouched in crimson, the hair of his body black, about to plunge. . . .

At some other time, though still in the same places, there used to be lots of genuine old public-houses. . . .

"Good puzzle," thinks Leopold Bloom, "would be cross Dublin without passing a pub."

. . . though, *these* plastic-coated days, they're now mostly something else again: guaranteed authentic reproductions, preserved

26

snugs and corners of gen-u-ine imitation local colour, stage-sets knocked-up by professionals for a continuous amateur performance of the traditional Comedy—which, on *these* creaking boards, is only the old Tragedy by its other name, Death wearing its other mask, the grin on the face of a corpse . . . faded and fading views of those "dear dead days beyond recall" . . . relics under glass, memories by the regulation pint, museums for the sale of Guinness, peep-shows for porter, animated cartoons to promote the consumption of bottled lamentation, the Three Star 70° proof tears of Cathleen ni Houlihan matured by craftsmen over the weary years. . . .

But never *pubs*.

Still plenty of them though, whatever they are. . . .

"In Dublin," says the Ginger Man, "you're never more than twenty paces from a pint."

Which is one way to be discovering Dublin for yourself, surely—to be taking those twenty paces as far as the open door of the nearest O'Rourke's or Kiernan's or Davy Byrne's. . . .

Where, says Hugh Kenner, "within memory of the bartender's father, the descent of the Irish Kings from Adam and of their language from the un-Babelized true names of the creatures in Eden was written out, with tables, in a thick green volume by a pious citizen."

And where, on the polished mahogany counter of the bar, standing on its own bleary reflection, will be this collecting-box for a Leper Mission run by the Holy Ghost Fathers in the Congo. . . .

An emotional and intellectual complex in an instant of time. . . .

. . . or, ringed from the standing of a pint, creased from being folded in a pocket, this marked programme of last night's greyhound racing at Shelbourne Stadium. . . .

"I tell you," says he who left it, "didn't every bloody dog I laid me money on run bloody lame on me!"

With everybody in earshot laughing and raising their glass as though for the first time to a flash of wit they have heard every morning after every night's racing at either Shelbourne Park *or* Harold's bloody Cross for the last twenty bloody years, so they have . . . and drinking up nice and slow, drawing it out by the book, spacing the mouthfuls, prolonging the agony till closing-time,

watching each other for the next move in the ritual, listening for the next invocation in the litany, laughing and weeping in this vale of *Lacryma Christi*, waiting for the next cue and the hour of their death. *Amen.*

"No," says the Citizen, eyeing the early knockings in the bottom of his late hours, "you can't beat a good pint of plain porter," says he, "a pint of plain is your only drink for a man, so it is."

> GUINNESS, the Celebrated National Beverage, *Ould Erin's Greatest Gift to the Drinking World*, being a rich dark Stout brewed from golden sun-ripened barley, fragrant hops, and natural yeast ... giving it the famous creamy head and the unique body.

> *Bless us, O Lord, and these Thy gifts,*
> *which we are about to receive from Thy*
> *bounty, through Christ our Lord. Amen.*

Unlike Scotch whisky, which is a blend, your true Irish is a pure and smooth pot-still whiskey (spelt with an 'e') of distinctive flavour. *ONCE TASTED, NEVER FORGOTTEN! ALWAYS INSIST ON REAL IRISH!*

It need hardly be stressed that it is *essential* for the preparation of genuine *Irish Coffee*: hot strong black coffee with plenty of brown sugar to taste, a stiff lacing with true Irish, topped with a good inch of cold thick fresh Irish cream!

"A pregnancy without joy," says young Stephen, having filled all cups that stood empty, "a birth without pangs, a body without blemish, a belly without bigness. Let the lewd with faith and fervour worship."

But, whatever you do, don't forget to bring home a bottle of *Irish Mist* with you—the world famous and equally distinctive Irish liqueur based on true Irish whiskey, selected herbs and aromatic spices, and natural Clover Honey from the "Four Fields" of Ireland . . . all subtly blended according to the stringent requirements of a Traditional Secret Recipe. . . .

> *We give Thee thanks, Almighty God, for*
> *all Thy benefits, Who livest and reignest,*
> *world without end.   Amen.*

"Dublin dry," says the Citizen, smacking his lips over the first sweet and bitter tastings of this new prospect before him, with the fresh pint to his fist and his own money still in his pocket, "Dublin dry," says he for the umpteenth time of his drinking life, nor will it be the last, not unless he dies this night, God forbid, "Dublin dry," says he, with never a man to deny him, "is Dublin dead."

May the souls of the Faithful departed, through the mercy of God, rest in peace. Amen.

And Dublin drunk, says I, having watched and listened and waited till after closing-time of a Saturday night, is Dublin disgusting, fighting mad and pig-stupid with it . . . pissing up against the nearest dark wall, shame the better part of dire necessity, spewing its porter into the nearest gutter, reeling across the wide-berthing pavements, unpredictable, bawling its sentimental songs of belligerence through tears of booze, spitting out its broken teeth with snot and obscenity. . . .

LAST BUS TO SANDYMOUNT. HADGROFT.

31

"Jesus bloody Christ!" says this bit of a young buck on the corner of South Lotts Road and Bridge Street, with the smell of it on him from yards away, and the last bus for Sandymount swept past full a good twenty minutes ago, "I'll be having that much of a bloody thick murdering head on me in the morning," says he, "it'll be the Devil's own job to shift me out of me bloody warm bed for Mass, so it will!"

And he belched a belch would wake the dead in Glasnevin Cemetery clear across the Liffey and the rest of Dublin. . . .

★　　★　　★

Which, by nothing stronger than association, reminds me of something one of my Aunts used to recite (if pressed) at parties:

> 'Twas an evening in November,
> As I very well remember,
> I was strolling down the street in drunken pride,
> But my knees were all a-flutter
> So I landed in the gutter—
> And a pig walked up and lay down by my side.
>
> Yes, I lay there in the gutter
> Thinking thoughts I couldn't utter,
> When a sweet Colleen did pass and softly say,
> "You can tell a man who boozes
> By the company he chooses."
> And the pig got up and trotted on its way!

Though, with what I now understand of the workings of Aunts, it was not so much a Party Piece as a comment from behind the back of her hand at the drinking of my Uncles, and them with all a decent drop taken.

And what would a pig be doing in the streets?

Well, don't the Irish still bring the creature to Market one day a week? and it with a string to its rear-leg for to be led?

32

After your night prayers what should you do?
After my night prayers I should observe due modesty in going to bed, occupy myself with the thoughts of death, endeavour to compose myself to rest at the foot of the Cross, and give my last thoughts to my crucified Saviour.

Which is another way to be discovering Dublin for yourself, just as surely—to be passing though the open door of the nearest Roman Catholic Church, remembering to make your confession of faith in Christ crucified by tracing a cruciform gesture on your body, touching your forehead, lower breast, left and right shoulders, with the tips of the fingers and thumb of the right hand held lightly together, accompanied by the words, *"In the Name of the Father, and of the Son, and of the Holy Ghost,"* having first taken a drop of Holy Water from the stoop you will find in some prominent position by the entrance. . . .

"I know by frequent experience," says the Blessed Saint Teresa of Avila, so she does, "that there is nothing which puts the devils of Hell to flight like Holy Water. They run away before the Sign of the Cross also," says she, "but they return immediately. Great then must be the power of Holy Water to put them to such flight."

Plenty of open doors to choose from. . . .

Indeed, would be an even better puzzle to cross Dublin without passing *six* churches or less than a dozen Priests—not counting Nuns or assorted Monks of various Orders.

"No," might say the Ginger Man, had he thought of it, "in Dublin you're never more than a genuflexion away from *some* sort of holiness."

Mind you, it's not the domesticated Roman Catholic holiness of your actual post-Christian England, but the sort to haunt the nightmares of the Papist-hating members of the Protestant Truth Society.

All the other usual sights and sounds and smells, of course. . . .

Ranks and ascensions and stands of candles and votive lights, gentle glimmerings and exultant blazings and constellations of

33

incandescence ... the pungency of hot wax and the lingerings of
incense on the cool inner air ... the swaying ruby gleaming of a
Sanctuary Lamp suspended from the mysterious upper darkness by
thin silver chains ... Altars and Altar Stones set with relics of Holy
Martyrs, Tabernacles for the reservation of the Blessed Sacrament,
Crucifixes, tinkling bells, all manner of Sacred Vessels made of gold
and silver: the Paten (on which is placed the Consecrated Host during
the Sacrifice of the Mass), the Chalice (which contains the Wine,
being the Blood of Our Redeemer's Passion and Death), the Ciborium
(larger than the Chalice, covered with a lid, in which are kept the
Sacred Hosts reserved for Holy Communion), and the Monstrance
(for the Exposition of the Blessed Sacrament to the view of the Faithful

MOORE STREET - DUBLIN. HANRAN?

34

at Benediction and during the Procession on the Feast of Corpus Christi) ... all manner of Sacred Vestments of linen and silk and cloth-of-gold, embroidered and enriched and stiff with encrustations: the Amice, the Alb, the Cincture (a symbol of Holy Purity), the Maniple, the Stole (a symbol of the dignity and power of the Holy Priesthood), and the Chasuble (a symbol of the Yoke of Christ) ... Liturgical colours to deepen the significance of the Seasons in the Church Year: White, signifying joy and Purity of Soul (used on the Feasts commemorative of the great events in the Life of Our Lord, on the Feasts of Our Lady, the Holy Angels, Confessors and Virgins), Red, the symbol of Fire and Blood (used at Pentecost and throughout Whitsuntide, on the Feasts of the Holy Martyrs, and on the days commemorative of the Sufferings of Our Blessed Redeemer), Green, the colour of Hope (used on the Sundays between Whitsuntide and Advent), Violet, symbolic of Penitence and Humility (used during Advent and Lent, on the Rogation Days, Ember Days, and Vigils of the Greater Feasts), Black, indicative of Sadness and Mourning (used on Good Friday, All Soul's Day, at Funeral Services, and in Masses for the Dead), with Rose permitted on Laetare Sunday in Advent and Gaudete Sunday in Lent ... all manner of statues, plain or coloured, in wood or stone or plaster or moulded plastic: the Cruci-fied, Our Blessed Lord of the Most Sacred Heart, His Holy Mother with the Child Jesus, Our Lady of the Seven Sorrows, Our Blessed Lady of the Immaculate Conception, the Blessed Virgin Mary as Star of the Sea, the Holy Mother of God as Mystical Rose, or as Queen of the Most Holy Rosary ... and all manner of Saints: the Blessed Saint Patrick himself, surely, the Patron Saint of Holy Ireland, and Saint Joseph, and Saint Teresa the Little Flower of the Child Jesus, and Saint Anthony of Padua with the Child Jesus, and Saint Bernadette of Lourdes, and Saint Francis of Assisi, and Saint Gerard Majella the Redemptorist, and. ...

"You've enough there", says he, "to be satisfying His Holiness the Pope himself, surely now?"

... and all the other Holy Apostles and Disciples and Martyrs and Bishops and Confessors and Learned Doctors of the Church and Priests and Religious and Hermits and Virgins and. ...

"Will you give over?" says he, *"or is it screaming bloody mad you want us this day?"*

... and, er, other Saints of God making intercession for us.

"Blessed be God!" says he, *"in His Angels and in His Saints!"*

But you'll see that sort of "inexplicable splendour," with only minor local variations, in Roman Catholic Churches all over the worshipping world: Dublin is its own City.

Second Colour-slide from a Set of Six

O'CONNELL STREET: Panoramic view, looking south from the top of the now destroyed Nelson's Pillar, with the dome of sky, the saucer-edge of blue-delft hills, the spires and cranes and new buildings, dove-grey stone and bleached cement, slates under the sun, windows glinting, the reds and greens and yellows of the cars like toys, rear-lights flashing and blinking, rhythmical rubies, Corporation buses Irish-green and some cream-white, other greens of distant trees and those below, crossings, the orange of the flowers along the middle of the bridge over the unseen Liffey, plinths and balustrades and balconies, pilasters and strips of flickering neon, ranks of chimneys, cupolas, a truck with a stack of brown barrels, a women with a straw-basket, a man selling papers ... and the statue of O'Connell himself, the Liberator, with his back to his street, but facing his bridge and the advertisements on the prow of the corner opposite ... *Gold Flake.* ...

At the other end of O'Connell Street, it says here, stands the Parnell Monument, a triangular shaft of Galway granite, 60 feet in height, erected in 1910 to the memory of Charles Stewart Parnell. ...

"Let him remember", cried Mr Casey, "the language with which the priests and the priests' pawns broke Parnell's heart and hounded him into his grave."

. . . with, on the pedestal, the bronze statue by the Irish-American sculptor, Augustin St Gaudens. . . .

NO MAN HAS THE RIGHT TO FIX THE BOUNDARY TO THE MARCH OF A NATION spell the letters of fine gold. . . .

Within spitting-distance are the open street-markets, stalls and barrows and stacks of boxes along the gutters, spuds by the pound from the sacks, carrots and spring-onions by the bunch, fish by the tail and still twitching in their slimy trays, the man slitting eels alive and scraping the guts into a bucket with the back of his knife, the pavements cracked and crowded, the voices in stereo, shouting the odds, naming the prices, calling the tune, with the people, *the people, yes*, out shopping, bargain-hunting, sauntering, pushing, shoving, side-stepping, orange-peel underfoot, baskets and bags on their arms, hats and caps and old black shawls on their heads, money in their pockets and purses, the pubs snug and thriving, ice-cream for the kids, or a chew of toffee to their gobs, bread and buns and stale cake cheaper than fresh, cuts of scrag-end of lamb, pork-chops and the inner organs of beasts and fowls ate with relish by Leopold Bloom, newspaper for the wrapping, the time of day to be passing, the dinner to be cooking and the smell of it already watering the mouth with hunger. . . .

Not that even Dublin shall live by tripe and cow-heel and ox-tail and liver and lights and kidneys and pig's trotters and tongue of sheep and cow alone, nor by all manner of any other offal . . . for there, on the corner of North Great George's Street, is this wheeled display-stand for the publications of the Irish Catholic Truth Society, Devotional, Historical, Doctrinal, Social, keeping abreast of the needs of the day. . . .

The Soviet Campaign Against God, The Catholic Mother, The Immaculate Conception of Our Blessed Lady, The Holy Rosary, Forbidden and Suspect Societies, Preparing Our Daughters for Life, A Talk to Catholic Wives, False Trends in Modern Teaching, Birth Control (Ethical, Social, and Medical Objections), The Fact of Hell, Private Morals and Public Life, A Modern Virgin Martyr (Saint Maria Goretti), What the Saints Looked Like. . . .

★　　　★　　　★

Consider Saint Gerard Majella the Redemptorist, previously mentioned, who, like Phlebas the Phoenician, "was once handsome and tall as you."

Though, perhaps, "handsome" is too strong a word for the face you'll see on his statues or the little Holy Picture cards you can buy for your Missal and Prayer Book: as soft as best Blue Band margarine, as gentle as Fairy Snow washing-up liquid, as girlish as the young Mary Pickford, with his big brown soulful eyes gazing tearfully Heavenwards to a far far sweeter home, his dainty little rosebud mouth quivering on the delicate brink of a shy little wistful smile, and his whole expression one of that simpering sort of piety usually reserved for heroines pining away of consumption or unrequited love in High Victorian Melodrama. . . .

"Isn't he the Darlin' Boy now!"

Outside Dublin and Holy Ireland the Church has to show better taste than to be spreading *that* brand of stuff all over our spiritual bread, and you'll not get much of *this* thickness of raspberry-jam either:

LITTLE GERARD AND LITTLE JESUS

In Muro, perched prettily on a slope of the Apennines, was Gerard born on the 6th April, 1726. The child, who was to ennoble and enrich a

pious father and mother beyond all their dreams, was God's most splendid gift to Dominico and Bernadetta Majella.

Precociousness is no rare thing in the Annals of Sanctity, and Jesus and Mary had indeed already taken possession of this young heart in a very wonderful way, and were not long in giving wonderful proofs of it. About a mile from the town was a Chapel in which an image of the Divine Mother and Her Child was venerated. One day the little boy, scarcely more than five, toddled out there alone. He knelt to pray. The Child of Bethlehem evidently saw something in that young heart yet lovelier than the mere sinlessness of childhood, for Gerard saw Him leave His Mother's arms and stand beside him. And then Mary's Son and Bernadetta's played together. When that wondrous play was ended, Gerard received from Jesus a tiny loaf of surpassing whiteness. Morning after morning was the prodigy renewed. Little Jesus seemed indeed to go out of His way to meet little Gerard, for the favoured boy was often given to feast his ravished eyes on the Divine Child on the altar after the Consecration. Wonderful happenings these, and yet who is going to set limits to what the Love of God may do when it meets with a Gerard?

His subsequent life has been spoken of as a "continuous miracle" and a "glittering chain of wonders." It is not our purpose to record these wonders in detail. It is enough to say that every gift and power we meet in other Saints we meet in Gerard. His frequent ecstasies were often witnessed by crowds, and more than once he was borne a long distance in what is known as ecstatic flight through the air. He had knowledge of the deepest personal secrets that amazed and terrified his audiences. At times he read the future like an open book. He knew of distant happenings, and displayed the rare gift of bilocation or being in two places at one and the same time. The elements obeyed him. The animal creation came and went at his beck. The Laws of Nature were often suspended at his bidding, as, for instance, in the sight of thousands, when he trod stormy waters in the Bay of Naples, and drew a sinking boat full of passengers to shore. Time and again food multiplied in his hands. On certain occasions he gave proof of the extraordinary power of making himself invisible. The bodily cures he effected are countless. He compelled the very demons of Hell to obey him. And he thirsted

39

for sufferings more than sinners thirst for pleasure. And how he did torture his own innocent body! Perhaps no Saint has surpassed Gerard in corporal austerities. Their details make for terrible and heart-rending reading. For instance, he. . . .

> *"Now you'll not be going into that like of agony, surely now?"*
> Yet *that's* the "distinctive flavour". . . .
> > *ONCE TASTED, NEVER FORGOTTEN!*
> > > . . . of Roman Catholic Dublin, most of the

men and women you'll pass on the streets believe every last miracle in hundreds of such accounts of other Saints, and you'll be asking for a quick fist in the bloody gob to argue too loudly about any of them in a public place—least of all within twenty paces of either a church *or* a pub. And *never* on Sundays!

★   ★   ★

Third Colour-slide from a Set of Six

ST STEPHEN'S GREEN: Crimson blossom in the trees fretted against the sky, inlays of intense sapphire, lapis lazuli mounted amidst the enamelled leaves and velvet shadows, the grass starred with fallen petals, planeted with daisies and sweet-wrappings, beds and squares and squads of yellow tulips, variegated orange, scarlet the colour of guardsmen, straggling lines of olive-green park-chairs punctuated by benches, people talking, the girls in their summer dresses, striped deck-chairs, blue and pink, the bust of Mangan on his plinth like a garden-god, pigeons, starlings, sparrows bouncing, a priest passing gravely, a girl skipping, her mother pushing the latest baby in the biggest pram you ever saw, the chrome shimmering on the spokes of the wheels, ducks in the sluggish water snatching at floating bread, gulls swooping, the dark reflections disturbed and gently fracturing and assembling again in liquid swirlings of silver and greens, the cigarette-ends drifting . . . and these two nuns side by side on a bench, one reading aloud from *The Cork Examiner*, and the other listening and knitting a shawl of black wool. . . .

Anyway, whatever the flavour of your true Irish Catholicism, there's no shortage of open doors through which to be trying it. . . .

St. Mary's Pro-Cathedral on Marlborough Street is, apparently, a "fine example of the Grecian-Doric style of architecture," and, it also says here, the "portico is a copy of the Temple of Theseus in Athens," so it is—which must be *some* sort of comment on Rome to please the Protestant Truth Society!

However, beneath this portico I was, as they say, "approached" by an old lady who reminded me of my dead grandmother . . . wore the same sort of long shapeless black dress, black shoes and stockings, with this black woollen shawl drawn over the white hairs of her head. . . .

"Excuse me, Sir," says she, with the wheedling of all Killarney to her voice, "could you be sparin' a few small coins," says she, "for there to be a Mass said in this place for the eternal rest of the immortal souls of me son taken from me in the war," says she, "and his father, a fine man, departed these eight months, which is a cryin' long time to be bearin' for any women, Sir. . . ."

And she gave me a look at their Memorial Cards, one nearly worn away with the handling since her Martin was taken, and it repaired with bits of sticky brown paper, and the other still clean and shiny except along the fold down the middle, both with the small photographs and the dates and the short prayers for the Dead and the verses. . . .

And so, for the sake of my grandmother, she got a few small coins out of me. . . .

(Not that I thought Mass would be doing the Dead much good.)

. . . and then a few out of the next man, a few more here and a couple elsewhere, unobtrusively, watching for who next, not everybody, rarely another women, a quick shuffle of steps forward, the quiet words spoken, and the easing away with blessings when the coins had been accepted. . . .

She was an artist, that old lady . . . and I stalked her from behind those Doric columns an hour or more, and it didn't break *my* heart when she moved on at the first stroke of noon to drink a glass of best and to count her takings in this little pub off the Cathal Brugha Street.

Lot of those Memorial Cards about, too.

Five inches by three, sometimes larger, sometimes smaller, folded down the middle to make a little booklet without pages, and you see them pinned up on notice-boards at the back of churches, and spreading to any spare woodwork, behind doors, on the sides of cupboards and confessionals, one lapping over another like leaves beneath a tree, generations of grief in their own turn being obscured by newer griefs, tearing and falling, cleared every so often to make room for more . . . not very well printed, mostly black and silver, the occasional green otherness of Ireland, with loopings of vaguely Celtic motives entwining and interweaving around the edges and the words, and a Cross and the *De Profundis* on the back, and, on the inside, the small square photograph of the Departed stuck into the space provided in the middle of a nest of prayers:

Blessed Saint Anthony pray for her

Sweet	Sweet
Heart	Heart
of	of
JESUS	MARY
be	be
Thou	Thou
her	her
Love	Help

O Sacred Heart of Jesus
Have Mercy on the Soul of
CATHERINE MORIARTY

And then the remainder of the available space filled with verses:

Your face is always before us,
Your voice we will never forget,
Your smile will linger forever,
In our memories we see you yet.

A light is from our household gone,
A voice we loved is stilled,
A place is vacant in our home
That never can be filled.

"Would be a hard man," says he, *"who wouldn't care if he was missed or not when his time came. . . ."*

(Seen in a shop-window: plaster and plastic statues of Jesus and Mary and all the standard saints in all their manifestations and sizes, plain or coloured or made to glow in the dark, medals, rosaries, scapulars, candles, votive lamps, pictures, plaques, cards, you name it.

And these gonks and trolls and cupie-dolls.)

Our Lady of Mount Carmel on Whitefriar Street. . . .
St Francis Xavier's on Gardiner Street. . . .
The Franciscan Church on Merchant's Quay, along the south bank of the Liffey almost opposite the Four Courts, where, one evening, out walking with my wife and children, we tried yet another open door. . . .

Marble, the radiance of candles, the great statue of the Blessed Virgin Mary high above the Main Altar circled with electric stars (one of them blown and out) . . . and the Brother to Saint Francis kneeling before Her and leading Her children in the saying of Her Holy Rosary: perhaps two or three hundred people, men and women, not many youngsters, all kneeling before the Queen of their Heaven with him, all telling their beads through the Decades, with him reciting the first part of each *Hail Mary* alone, and all of them reciting the second part in straggling unison. . . .

"Where," whispered my wife, a life-long Protestant and, despite her background and beliefs, stangely moved by this sort of thing, "where in England," she whispered, "would you be able to find this number of people willing to come out on a week-night to go to church?"

But, with having come out myself on I don't know how many week-nights in times past to this very church for Benediction and the Rosary, I had the ear to know that the Franciscan was gabbling, running the words together in clusters like the beads through his restless fingers. . . .

> *"Hail-Mary-full-of-grace the-Lord-is-with-thee*
> *blessed-art-thou-among-women and-blessed-is-the-fruit*
> *of-thy-womb-Jesus. . . ."*

. . . obviouly getting through them (words *and* beads) against the clock (he even glanced at his wristwatch a chance or two, this Brother to Saint *Francis* wearing a *wristwatch*), starting the first part of the next *Hail Mary* a phrase before the congregation had properly finished their part of the previous one. . . .

> "Holy Mary, Mother of God, pray for us sinners. . . ."

And off he'd go at nineteen to the cantering dozen. . . .

> *"Hail-Mary-full-of-grace. . . ."*

. . . with them still seconds behind, floundering. . . .

> ". . . now, and at the hour of our death, Amen. . . ."

. . . tailing away, confused, losing the rhythm . . . and I was disappointed, embarrassed, a bit ashamed on behalf of those around me whose Faith I once shared, wanting the recitation to sound better (if only as a more coherent public performance, an oratorio without

45

music, a mere piece of choral speaking without any thought of its value as prayer), wanting to justify the days and stories of my boyhood, to have my wife see and hear the best of these things, to show her that Irish Catholicism wasn't like *this* in those times past. . . .

(Though, of course, it often *was*.)

Until, eventually, after a few more laps, even she couldn't help but notice, and gave me a look that needed an answer.

We didn't have long to wait for one.

The last words were gotten through like shot from a shovel, himself left the steps of the Altar with his "duty all ended" . . . there was a moment of relative quiet . . . and there then was the usual superficially reverent scramble for the aisles and out. . . .

Except that we, and a few other apparent noncomformists, those heading towards the Main Doors for Merchant's Quay, seemed to be on our own, no pushing, no shoving, natural resisters with nothing to resist, no stream congesting before the stoops of Holy Water, no wilderness of frustration between us and the milk and supper of Dublin . . . whilst everybody else and their friends and relations and the ould Biddy who lives round there on the corner off Cook Street were all crowding out through the side doors, so they were, and having a not quite good-natured jostling time of it. . . .

"Where are they going?" said the children. "It's much easier *this* way, isn't it?"

"Must be yet another little quirk of the Irish Character," says

herself, "which your father will undoubtedly explain as soon as he can think of something plausible enough."

This I ignored—as what man wouldn't a remark the like of that?

And we came out into the evening again, the City serene across the Liffey as though the background in a fresco by Giotto, some incident from the Life of the Blessed Saint Francis, with himself likely along any minute . . . the light with that gentle clarity you'll not see anywhere else but on those rare and silver days, the sun dissolving behind the trees of Phoenix Park, westering, transmuting . . . a few stars already gleaming, a necklace of street-lamps already strung along the river and reflecting, shimmering in the hither-and-thithering waters of. . . .

Next door to the church, in the Hall, there was *BINGO TONIGHT*.

"When boring through a mountain from two sides," says Shem the Penman, "the question is," says he, "how to meet in the middle."

And there are more than two sides to Dublin.

So we went for a walk around the back-doubles, and managed to

47

be sort of passing by as they came crowding out through those different doors. . . .

'Bad cess to me luck!" says this women, "Wasn't I just the one damn number short on that last card?"

. . . and, for the sake of those days and stories of my boyhood, we got talking to the young Brother to Saint Francis who'd been an envigilator up there on the platform inside, checking the numbers drawn against the numbers called, with the smell of the tobacco-smoke on him from yards away and him taking a turn or two along the Quay for a breath of good air, so he was, tall, tonsured, the brown cloth of his habit coarse and fraying, the lilt of Galway to his voice. . . .

"Tell us," we said, after the usual hesitations and introductions, "how do you think Saint Francis would react to all this?"

And we walked and talked an hour or so along by those waters, and he told us about Assisi where he'd been studying these last four years, with this his first week home in Ireland, and how the Umbrian landscape had taught him to see Saint Francis in a new light, discover new facets to his character, new ways of looking at the old old problems of sin and human need . . . and he told us about his own life, and Galway, and the call of Saint Francis to his own heart, and of the Missions to Africa where he believed his vocation was, and of their great needs, and the desperate shortage of money. . . .

And he smiled . . . 'Where else would it come from?" he said, "if not from this place and the hearts of these people?"

And we hadn't the heart, nor the hatred, to argue with him. . . . and we listened and walked and he told us about his love of God, and Our Blessed Lord, and of Our Lady . . . and he was one of those with the Light shining out of them, and he blessed us and our children. . . .

(Not that we thought the blessing of any man would be doing us much good, but that God would bless us all through such giving and receiving of a gift of love.)

. . . and we thanked him, and shook hands, and said Goodnight, and walked on back towards where we were staying, and turned on the corner of Bridge Street, and we all waved Goodbye to him where

48

he waited in the light of a street-lamp across the Quay, and I'll never forget him.

But he had no answer to convince himself, let alone us.

Please forgive us, Brother Bernard—for we did not ask in love.

St Teresa's Carmelite Church on Clarendon Street. . . .

St Paul's on Arran Quay. . . .

St Mary's on. . . .

"You've enough there," says he, "to be contenting His Eminence the Cardinal Archbishop of All Ireland himself, surely now?"

St Mary's on Haddington Road. . . .

"There's a church of that name in Rathmines," says he, "but enough's a bloody enough!"

Well, er, yes, that's true . . . though there are, it says here, "quite a considerable number of others throughout the length and breadth of the City, catering for all shades of belief and classes of men."

Holy Water and plain porter, then, exposition and drama, the allegedly Sacred and the so-called Profane, centripetal and centrifugal, now running parallel, now entwined, "confused patterns . . . whose convolutions seem alternatively to seek and avoid each other. . . ."

> *O Ireland my first and only love*
> *Where Christ and Caesar are hand and glove!*

"I am afraid," says this same exile with the black patch over his left eye, and him talking to a critical feller by the name of Cyril Connolly, and it all printed for the world to see in the literary pages of the *New Statesman*, and somebody's leg being pulled as though

ANNE STREET. DUBLIN. HOLDCRAFT ?

it had bells on, "I am more interested in the Dublin street names than in the riddle of the universe."

Though, as always, his "running riddle" has its own "fluid answer" in the long Litany of sounds and echoes. . . .

Abbey, Amiens, Annamoe, Aughrim. . . .

(More like a declension that a list, surely!)

Ballybough, Belvedere, Blackhorse, Black Pitts, Bridgefoot, Brunswick, Burlington. . . .

(The past crying aloud from the rooftops of the present. Agreed, a stale image—but how fresh is the Dublin past?)

Cabra, Camden, Capel, Cathal Brugha. . . .

(Acting President of the first Assembly of Ireland, appointed on the 21st January, 1919, after the Irish Republican victory at the polls in the so-called "Khaki Election." Took a leading part (with Michael Collins, Liam Lynch, Rory O'Connor, Liam Mellows, and Erskine Childers) in the war of resistance against English attempts to overthrow the new Irish State by force of arms and the savage use of the notorious Black-and-Tans. In the Civil War which followed the Truce and Treaty of 1921 he was (with Michael Collins, Liam Lynch, Rory O'Connor, Liam Mellows, and Erskine Childers) murdered by his fellow Irish Republicans. R.I.P.)

Davitt, D'Olier, Dominick, Drumcondra. . . .

Earlsfort, Eccles. . . .

("The blind of the window was drawn aside" upstairs at Number Seven. "A plump bare generous arm shone, was seen, held forth from a white petticoatbodice and taut shiftstraps. A woman's hand. . . ."

Another epiphany.

Thou still unravish'd bride. . . .)

Fairview, Fenian, Fishamble, Foley. . . .

Gardiner, Grafton, Granby. . . .

Hanover, Harcourt, Harold's Cross, Henrietta, Hogan, Holles. . . .

("The Lying-in Hospital in Holles Street is to be distinguished from the Mater Misericordiae in Eccles Street, as most Catholic funerals pass the latter on their way to the neighbouring cemetery, whilst the former, the House of Life, is more cheerfully situated on

the road leading to the Royal Dublin Society Horse Show at Balls-bridge.")

Innisfallen, Irishtown. . . .

("Brothels," says William Blake, "are built with the bricks of religion," and there was never a truer word said.)

James and John. . . .

Kevin, Kildare, Killarney, Kilmainham. . . .

("Where," our Uncle Mike would say, "in the stone-breaking yard of the jail, the Martyrs of the Easter Rising were shot down with British guns! Let you never be forgetting that!")

Lansdowne, Leeson, Leinster. . . .

(Ulster, Leinster, Munster, Connacht—are these not the Four Fair Fields of Ireland?)

Mangan, Mary's Lane, Meath, Merchant's Quay, Merrion, Mountjoy. . . .

New Row, Northbrook, North Wall. . . .

O'Connell, O'Donovan, Old Cabra, Ormond. . . .

Parnell and Pearse. . . .

("But the fools, the fools! They have left us our Fenian dead!

While Ireland hold these graves, Ireland unfree will never be at rest!")

Raglan and Ranelagh, Rathdown and Rathmines, Ringsend and Ross. . . .

Sandymount, Sean McDermott. . . .

(Shot with James Connolly on 12th May, 1916, in that stone-breaking yard which enclosed the nightmares of my childhood.)

. . . Shelbourne, Simmonscourt, Slievenamon, Stoneybatter. . . .

Talbot, Tara. . . .

Usher, Vincent, Wexford, Wicklow, Wolfe Tone Quay. . . .

Who needs riddles with names the like of that? Who needs the universe when the street-map of Dublin may be read as the cracked mirror of Man?

But what sort of doublin' blather does it mention here for the convenience of Visitors to this gay, debonair, delightful, distinctive, friendly, warm-hearted, generous, impulsive, various, devious, dangerous, roistering, rowdy, relaxed and lapsing top of the mornin' Erin mavourin of an ould Darlin' Cushla-ma-Chree of all our achin' hearts?

Sea Routes, Air Terminal, Banks, Buses and Coaches, Distances, Early Closing and Market Days, Entertainments (including *Cinemas, Concerts,Dancing,Night Clubs,*and *Theatres*), *Hotels and Accommodation. . . .*

London, Paris, Rome, Berlin, Madrid, New York, Los Angeles, Rio . . . with the same concrete beginning to spread over the shamrock. . . .

Fourth Colour-slide from a Set of Six

OPEN-AIR BOOK STALLS ON THE QUAYS: Sagging shelves of secondhand junk about this and that and all seven sorts of the other, stacked and packed and piled or standing, or sliding sideways into empty spaces, Folio, Quarto, Octavo, the long, the short, the fat Demy, the slim volume, old and older, tattered, split, littered, divided, uncut, unopened, unread, dog-eared, cat-scratched, dusty, faded with days of sun, spotted with ancient rain, stained, strained, fingered, rubbed, borrowed, stolen, lost, abandoned, crumbled leather or fraying cloth or paperback giving up all hope, thrillers, chillers, sermons by the weary hour, autobiographies by the forgotten, novels, essays, epics, lyrics, histories, mysteries, poems, verses, plays, lays, lies, politics, Kings' Treasuries . . . and this young man leafing through *Steps to Christ. . . .*

★   ★   ★

"Will you listen now?" says this man I was listening to on O'Connell Street, "but what's that building across there?"

"The General Post Office," says I, with no need of a Guide Book to me hand at all.

"It is that," says he, "Heart of the Easter Rising, where the feet of our Noble Martyrs have trod . . . Well now, would you know who's bought that site next to it?"

I'd read it in the papers that very morning, so I had, but he looked the sort of man who'd want to be first with news the like of that, so I gave him a shrug merely, and left him the field.

"Marks and Spencers!" says he. "Would you believe that?"

He didn't look the sort of man you'd contradict, either: "Well," says I, "there's been talk of it being the British Home Stores. . . ."

"And what would be the difference?" says he, "with the Freedom our Fathers Fought and Died For within Living Memory being sold back for Thirty Pieces of Tarnished Silver!"

And I'm *still* not sure whether or not he was habilitating himself for the Coming War of Liberation, or having me on.

But, for all that, he spat into the gutter quite convincingly: "There," says he, "*that* for what they're doing to this country!"

Though so help me, wasn't he wearing a casual blue sports shirt the like of which you can only be getting in Marks and Spencers?

And why wouldn't he? With them being the bargains they are?

Which is a question only he could answer—though, again, he didn't look to be the sort of man to be asking.

★ ★ ★

Though, while we're in O'Connell Street, did you ever hear of the last end of Lord Nelson?

Well, at one time of the British day, bang in the middle of O'Connell Street for every Patriotic citizen to see, bold as you like and twice as randy, there used to be the Nelson Pillar, so there did—which, it says here, "was the city's best-known landmark, having been erected in 1808 to a height of 134 feet, from the top of which an excellent panoramic view of Dublin and its environs could be obtained for the payment of a small admission fee."

"Not to mention the climbing of more bloody stairs than Jacob's ladder ever had," says himself. . . .

"Nelson," says Stephen Dedalus, "the one-handled adulterer."

"One-handled adulterer," says Professor MacHugh. "That tickles me, I must say."

"Tickled the old ones, too," says Myles Crawford, Ruler of the Winds of Rhetoric, "if the God Almighty's truth was known."

So, with it an affront to Morality and *Irish* Patriotism (or something), the top half was blown-off one loyal night by a suitcase of Gaelic gelignite left on those stairs inside. . . .

Though (*verbum sat sapienti*) there'll be no questions about who had the leaving of that suitcase.

Blown-off as neat as a sliced candle, it was, with hardly a pane of glass broken in the shops of the street, just the rubble by the ton, and it blocking the way in all directions. . . .

"And didn't some smart feller nip in and lift Nelson's bloody head," says himself. . . .

Leaving the base and the bottom half of it standing there like a spare at a wedding, neither one thing nor the other. . . .

"I heard he got a good price," says himself. . . .

So it was decided to blow the rest up, as the cost of demolition was tendered for and found not to be worth what the rubble would fetch. . . .

"Should have tried selling it to the American who bought that bloody head," says himself. . . .

And they called in the Irish Army, being the experts when it came to the handling of explosives. The area was cleared, the charges laid, and up it went . . . and blew out every window this side of the Liffey.

"Should have left the bloody job to the boys who had the starting of it," says himself. . . .

Anyway, back to the doublin' blather again:

. . . *Postal Information*, *Restaurants* (including *American Style, Chinese, French, German, Indian, Irish Traditional*, and *Italian*), *Sports* (including *Athletics, Bowling, Boxing, Fishing, Gaelic Football, Golf, Greyhound Racing, Hockey, Horse Racing, Hurling, Polo, Rowing, Rugby Football, Show Jumping, Soccer, Swimming, Tennis,* and *Wrestling*), *Stations*, and (so help me) *Interesting Facts:*

> *POPULATION* (including Suburbs, Environs, and the
> Borough of Dun Laoghaire) 663,389

A figure which, by all Natural Law and relevant Papal Encyclicals, and with the public sale of contraceptives prudently forbidden by Civil Law for the sake of Civic fruitfulness and the Greater Glory of God, *ought* to have increased and multiplied even *during* the count, let alone since.

(*"You're wrong there," says he, "for isn't there the Bill proposed in the Dial to be changing that?"*)

Except, of course, that all a man need be doing is slip in for a short back and sides from a barber who knows you well enough. . . .

"Will that be *all*, Sir?" he'll say as he brushes you down and panders you up afterwards—and there'll be this bit of a nod and a wink at the drawer where he stocks the *Durex.* . . .

Or you'll know this likely lad with a brother working in England on the motor-cars or the building. . . .

"Sure, doesn't Kevan himself post 'em back home when there's call?"

And then, again (an *Interesting Fact* you'll not often heard mentioned at home in these modest Suburbs and Environs), your Irish Colleen who so far forgets herself as to offer a particular insult to the Immaculate Mother of God, Mary, ever a Virgin, by daring to commit either a Mortal or a Venial sin against the Sixth Commandment. . . .

What is Mortal Sin?

Mortal sin is a grievous offence against God, and it is called Mortal sin because it kills the soul by depriving it of sanctifying grace, and deserves Hell.

Where will they go who die in Mortal Sin?

They who die in Mortal sin will go to Hell for all eternity, where the wicked shall live and be punished for ever in the fire.

What is Venial Sin?

Venial sin is an offence which does not kill the soul, yet displeases God, and often leads to Mortal sin and its fearful consequences.

What is the Sixth Commandment?

The Sixth Commandment is, 'Thou shalt not commit adultery,' and it forbids all sins of impurity and unchaste freedom with another's wife or husband.

Does the Sixth Commandment also forbid whatever else is contrary to Holy Purity and Chastity?

The Sixth Commandment also forbids whatever else is contrary to Holy Purity and Chastity, such as all immodest thoughts, looks, words, actions, dances, songs, discourses, articles, books, novels, verses, pictures, statues, photographs, films, and television programmes, and it is sinful to enjoy, permit, condone, tolerate, or profit from them. . . .

. . . and gets herself pregnant outside of Holy Matrimony, and then can't persuade the dirty devil of him to honour his moral obligations, is traditionally obliged by Priest and Family to forsake her Native Land, and to have her baby or abortion in Liverpool or London.

"Mother of God!" says he, "you'll be telling the Dark Rosaleen she's the bloody Whore of Babylon next, so you will!"

Possibly, but. . . .

"To be insulting the Purity of Irish Girlhood!"

Well, though it would be a bold man, for an example on a slightly lower level of emotion, to be telling his wife she's getting wrinkles, is she any the less loved for having them?

"It's a known fact that the Irish Girl is the Sweetest Purest Creature of the Western World!"

And isn't it the blind women who doesn't know she's got them?

"So," says he, "if you'll be taking a word of advice. . . ."

All of which means, obliquely, that to be telling Dublin what Dublin doesn't want to hear is rather like. . . .

"Aren't you the bloody persistent man!"

"To the tourist,
This land may seem a dreamland, an escape,
But to her sons—and even more her daughters—
A dream from which they yearn to wake. . . ."
(Thank *you*, Louis MacNeice.)

Right, then—back to safer ground amongst those *Interesting Facts*:

George Frederick Handel, disappointed in London, and "driven by the Goddess of Dullness to the Hibernian Shore," discovered appreciation in the gay, brilliant, eccentric Society of the Irish Capital, and composed his *Messiah* to "offer this generous and polished Nation something new," it being first performed at the Musick Hall, Fishamble Street, on the 13th April, 1742, with Handel himself conducting, where it attracted a large and distinguished audience crowded with famous names, his visit being no isolated event, whilst, in 1745, was founded the Rotunda, the world's oldest Maternity Institution, which attracts students from many countries, though the Dublin Zoo, noted for its success in the breeding of lions, may merely lay claim to the the third oldest Institution of its kind, with, however, Phoenix Park, laid out by the Duke of Ormond as a hawking ground for the Viceroys, having a circumference of seven miles, undoubtedly being the largest enclosed public park in the world. . . .

"Well," says he, "would you know something else about the Phoenix Park now? The infantry of the Dublin Castle Garrison used to be marching across the green grass of that place in the very scarlet tunics worn at the famous Battle of Waterloo in the year of eighteen-fifteen, with many a man walking the streets of Dublin this day whose grand-father had watched them drilling and stamping as a boy. Isn't that the touch of history, surely?"

It is that, with the Wellington Monument within its purlieus most certainly being the world's highest obelisk, and with the Guinness Brewery, site of the Western Gate of the Mediaeval walled city, unmistakably the world's. . . .

But who needs to finish that sort of list?

"What you have omitted to mention," says this gent in a bowler-hat "is the indubitable circumstance of the Dublin Chamber of Commerce having been in continuous existence since the year seventeen-eighty-three, thus making it the. . . ."

"Wouldn't that be the dictionary under his hat now!"

Or there's the Literature bit:

Comprising Essayists, Miscellaneous, Novelists, Playwrights, and *Poets* (including *Brendan Behan, Padraic Colum, William Congreve, Lord Dunsany, Sheridan Le Fanu, Oliver St John Gogarty, Oliver Goldsmith, Lady Gregory, Charles Lever, James Clarence Mangan, George Moore, Thomas Moore, Flann O'Brien, Sean O'Casey, George Bernard Shaw, Richard Brinsley Sheridan, James Stephens, Jonathan Swift, John Millington Synge, Oscar Wilde,* and *William Butler Yeats*). . . .

The whole place littered with the wordy sons and daughters of. . . .

A memorial tablet at Number 12 Aungier Street denotes the house, now a pub, in which Thomas Moore, the darling of London's drawingrooms, was born in 1779, his father being in business here as a grocer and spirit dealer. . . .

Saw this middle-aged man dandering along Aungier Street early one Sunday morning, hardly anybody else about . . . only those on their glad way to the first Mass of the resurrecting week, and wandering strangers and returning sons the likes of me, and our footsteps echoing through the dreams behind all the curtained windows upstairs. . . .

Though *he* woke no dreamer, save himself.

Tall, gaunt, a jerking marionette with more than his strings tangled, his hands conducting the Adagio of some Romantic Symphony, perhaps Brahms or Mahler, or perhaps he was arranging the long white flowing robes draping the feet of Almighty God?

A busman's peaked-cap to his head, a British army greatcoat open and flapping, the brass buttons greenly neglected, what looked like an old red velvet waistcoat over a grey wollen cardigan for shirt, and what used to be white cricket-trousers tucked into folded-down wellingtons, and this Trinity College scarf bannering him fore and aft. . . .

Talking to himself, quietly, privately. . . .

Caught the few words in passing:

". . . one little while and then no more. . . ."

Vaguely familiar, heard them somewhere before. . . .

But where?

And he suddenly turned right down York Street on his way to Heaven or Saint Stephen's Green. . . .

"Every now and then," wrote Yeats, "when something has stirred my imagniation, I begin talking to myself. I speak in my own person and dramatise myself, very much as I have seen a mad old women do upon the Dublin quays, and sometimes detect myself speaking and moving as if I were still young, or walking like an old man with fumbling steps."

Do we wake or dream?

Who are the mad when there are Poets still dandering the streets?

Yet, though most of them left, and many of us still leave, "fearful

61

of its seduction, ashamed of its sordidness, weary of its envy, disgusted with its futility," all carry it like a ragbag stuffed with the sweepings of the Seventh City of Christendom, useful to neither man nor priest, too meretricious to keep, too much bloody trouble to sort out for junking.

But for the one. . . .

Old father, old artificer, stand me now and ever in good stead.

"James Joyce?" said this English student of English Literature at Trinity College. . . .

(Though just how chauvinistic can you get? With a list of names the like of *that* in the index under "English" Literature!)

. . . and this on top of the bus out to Sandymount. . . .

"Well," he said, "one hears a lot of him at lectures and seminars, naturally, along with Yeats, and I've sort of discussed him with two or three friends, that sort of thing—but, to be honest, I can't actually remember him being mentioned much at all anywhere else." And then he laughed: "Though I've heard more about politics in the last months than I've heard in the rest of my life! Don't they *ever* talk about anything else at all in pubs?"

The *James Joyce Museum* is in the Martello Tower which, it *almost* says here, "figures in his famous work, *Ulysses*, and the film of the same name, and was also his own residence for a time" . . . out there on the southern swerve of shore and bend of Dublin Bay off the Coast Road to Dun Laoghire where, with himself surely, you can walk into eternity a way a lone a last a loved a long that Sandymount Strand. . . .

(*Frequent buses from O'Connell Street.*)

The Tower, it also *does* say here, "is now a permanent Joyce Centre, and contains a number of first editions, books, manuscripts, records, portraits, letters, photographs, personal mementoes, and the death mask."

MARTELLO TOWER. SANDYCOVE.

The death mask . . . ghostly light on the metallic persona. . . .

It hangs on the whitewashed wall, bronze by gold ectoplasm, as green as the snotgreen sea rimming the sky between the Hill of Howth and Dalkey, finally sightless in silence, timeless in some other Tara, finally empty of all that commodius vicus of recirculating words. . . .

How small it's all!

. . . finally certain of. . . .

Tell me, tell me, tell me, elm!

. . . the four last things to be ever remembered. . . .

> *What are the four last things to be ever remembered?*
> The four last things to be ever remembered are Death, Judgement, Hell, and Heaven. . . .

. . . finally celebrating that one long Wake from which. . . .

"Isn't it the truth I've told ye?"

. . . even he will have to wake again.

Old Father, Our Mother, all sins and laughters of . . . *Amen.*

63

Fragment of an Imaginary Literary Conversation

"Will you wait now?"

"What for? Only there's this Big Scene building up, and, er—well. . . ."

"That Literature bit awhile back. . . ."

"What about it?"

"You mentioned George Moore and Thomas Moore. . . ."

"As who wouldn't in any representative list of. . . ."

"And Flann O'Brien?"

"Didn't Graham Greene himself call *At Swim-Two-Birds* a book in a thousand? and Philip Toynbee say that if he. . . ."

"But no mention of. . . ."

". . . were cultural dictator in England. . . ."

"Which God forbid!"

". . . he'd make it compulsory reading in all our universities? And didn't V. S. Pritchett say that he. . . ."

"No mention of the *other* O'Brien."

"Come again?"

"Edna."

"But you surely can't expect to be including every. . . ."

"Born in County Clare, which makes her as Irish as the rest of 'em!"

"Well, er. . . ."

"Short stories, novels, television plays, films—what more has the woman to do? With some set in Dublin, Holy Mother Church an influence, and Kingsley Amis awarding her first novel his personal. . ."

"Right, then! Edna O'Brien it is!"

"I believe," says she, with herself talking to Nell Dunn, and the whirring of a tape-recorder distinctly audible, "I believe," says she, so she does, "in only one or two sins, cruelty, killing, injustice. These are sins," says she, "everything else, lust, sex, adultery, covetousness are venial, you know," says she, "they're just little flaws."

"Well, now, won't *that* be pleasing some we could name in Dublin!"

"Satisfied?"

"Justice has been rendered."

"This, er, Big Scene?"

"Let you be sparing nothing. . . ."

64

So: *Once upon a time and a very good time it was there was a. . . .*

The wallpaper blue, with pink roses . . . and I remember, I remember the big china chamber-pot under the bed of a night, with the rim of it cold to our bums. . . .

And the cane always hanging behind the bedroom door . . . though they were not the good times. . . .

But curling up in the old armchair by the fire in the kitchen, with the red glowing caverns of Hell safe behind the bars of the grate, the heat tight as fever on my face. . . .

And rashers of bacon frying on the griddle, and the weight of the cat limp and warm and purring in my lap, and the window open to the sounds of the street, and the brown lino in the passage, and the knocker with the face of a lion on the front door, and the whiteness of the step when it had just been hearth-stoned. . . .

And my grandmother:

She had this smell of damp ashes and moth-balls, would wear a big white pinafore over her long shapeless black dress, borne the six sons (Uncle Bill and Uncle Martin of them in America) and the three daughters (one our mother), and would likely have had more but Himself died, took a jug round the corner for the half-quart'n of draught Guinness six days of the week (but for Sundays, when our Uncle Mike or our Uncle Danny would be bringing her a drop of

65

something in a bottle, so they would) . . . she'd wear this black hat with the purple silk ribbon and flowers of dark red felt to it for Mass on Sundays and Holy Days of Obligation, and these great long hatpins like she'd be stabbing through to her brain—but for the jug round the corner there'd be this black woollen shawl drawn over the white hairs of her head . . . and she'd keep this jug on a shelf in the kitchen, covered with a piece of cloth like the Purificator on the Chalice at Mass, except that it was sewn along the hem with blue beads for weight enough to keep it from blowing off every time the back door was opened on the wind from the sea, to be keeping out the dust and the flies. . . .

"When would you see a fly with a drink taken?" our Uncle Mike would say. "Can't they be telling what it's done to the likes of me?"

. . . and she'd be taking a sup when she'd a mind to . . . and she always kept half a lemon on a saucer for to soften the corns of her feet, and this bottle of Holy Water on the chair by her bed, and she'd pass from room to room during thunder-storms, sprinkling— she had this little china stoop given her by the Priest she'd worked for as a scullery-maid before she got married at sixteen in Connemara, that had the green leaves on it, and the red flowers, and the Sacred Heart of Jesus aflame for the love of us poor banished children of Eve, so it was . . . and she'd pass from room to room sprinkling us and the house from this stoop, and at every flash of lightning she'd cross herself, and at every crack of thunder she'd mumble the *Prayer for a Good Death*. . . .

"O Jesus, Mary, and Joseph," we'd be hearing, "I give you my heart and my soul . . . O Jesus, Mary, and Joseph, assist me in my last agony. . . ."

"It's not *you* suffering the agony, Mother," our Uncle Mike would say, "with it wetter inside this house than it is out there on the street for *all* the rain!"

And then our own mother would give him a look would have skinned a cat, and we'd none of us let on we'd heard him. . . .

"Kate," he'd say, "you're as bad as herself!"

And our mother. . . .

"And what is death?" asked Buck Mulligan, "your mother's or yours or my own?"

(Have *I* crossed her last wish in death?)

She had a Special Devotion to the Blessed Saint Anthony of Padua with the Child Jesus, had his statue in her room, his Brief and Medal in a tiny embroidered sachet around her neck. . . .

St Anthony's Brief, or Letter, is a piece of paper with these words:

> *"Ecce crucem Domini. Fugite partes adversae. Vicit Leo de Tribu Juda, Radix David, Alleluia. Alleluia."*

It is worn by the Faithful as a protection against evil, spiritual and temporal, for this Great Saint, one of the brightest ornaments of the Franciscan Order, has justified and confirmed all devotion paid to him by his willingness to plead with success before the Throne of God, and to help the unfortunate in any difficulty and to have compassion on the sorrows of the poor.

. . . and his Lilies in a slightly larger embroidered sachet which she kept in the back of her purse and took with her every time she went out, and transferred to her best handbag for Mass on Sundays and. . . .

By a special Papal Dispensation the Franciscan Fathers have the great privilege of Blessing the White Lily on the Feast of the Saint (13th June) as a reminder of his spotless and Heroic Chastity, and the Faithful often carry a treasured portion about their person in

order to obtain relief from illness, or to overcome temptation against
Holy Virtue. Many remarkable cures have been wrought by the. . . .

Wanted me to be a Priest, to be a good boy, a credit to her, to say
my first Mass for the Perpetual Rest of her Immortal Soul, to . . . .

With, always . . . hanging behind the bedroom door, the . . .
always. . . .

  O Clement, O Loving, O Sweet Virgin Mary . . .
  . . . why did it have to be always?

    Kyrie eleison
    Christe eleison
    Kyrie eleison

★ ★ ★

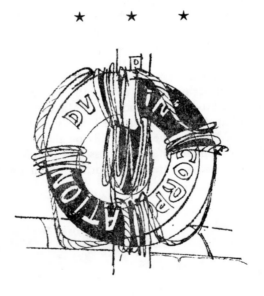

Fifth Colour-slide from a Set of Six
 THE PORT OF DUBLIN: The smudged sky and the distant
freedom of the sea, the Liffey at last almost swerving to that enfabled
bend of bay, with there the Grand Canal Dock and Alexandra Basin,

there the Lighthouse at the butt of the enclosing wall, with the moored ships between and behind the sheds and wharves and roofs, everywhere the flags and banded funnels, black and red and dirty white, squares, stripes, triangles, the dipping cranes, chains, cobbles, crates, rust and paint and the oil smearing the green water with metallic sheening, scum and dried froth lining stone with the depth of the morning tide, bilges emptying and splashing, steam hissing, the throbbing of engines, the smell of diesel, the gulls screaming, whistles, lowerings and hoistings and dischargings and clankings, grids and girders, shadows, wires and ropes and hawsers, sacks, hooks, derricks, men bending and heaving, bales and timber and imported cars, tankers from the Gulf, coasters, tugs, a man swabbing down a deck, spitting over the rail . . . and a boy watching from the near corner of Sir John Rogerson's Quay. . . .

But loaves of soda bread hot and steaming from the griddle . . . and fat coins of butter like the gold sovereign on our father's watch-chain, pale yellow and floating in the water of the earthenware dish, and them embossed with the shamrock by the little wooden paddles and moulds my grandmother would let me use when I'd been good or to make it up to me after our mother had been taking the. . . .

"Christ!" our Uncle Mike would say, "will you look at the state of him now? Surely," he'd say, with me at the sink in the kitchen, and my grandmother washing the tears from my face with her own flannel and a drop of hot water from the kettle, "it'll be a bloody miracle if I don't take that bloody thing to be laying it across her own fine fat arse one of these bloody days, so I bloody will!"

"Whisht!" my grandmother would say, "will you not keep a still tongue to your head, man! It's not for the likes of you to be interfering!"

"*Interfere?*" our Uncle Mike would say. "Why that father of his doesn't put his hand on her I'll never. . . ."

"Whisht now!" my grandmother would say, nearly drying the skin from my ears with the towel. . . .

69

And our Uncle Mike would pretend to be clipping me a back-hander for the side of me head, so he would. . . . "Though I'll not be saying you didn't deserve it!" he'd say to me, and find a penny in his pocket for something from the shop round the corner. . . .

And then my grandmother would take out the little wooden paddles and moulds from the drawer to the dresser, and I'd mint the butter with the leaves of shamrock, so I would . . . or she'd set me to kneel in front of the fire with a leg of ham to be browning, spooning the glaze of demerara sugar from its little iron saucepan to run like glistening rivers and fan out into descending lakes and seas of sweetness. . . .

"Glory be!" my grandmother would say, "there's more going into your greedy mouth than where I'm wanting it this very minute!"

. . . or she'd stand me on the stool by the sink to be slicing the onions for the stew. . . .

"If I'm to be having tears in this kitchen," she'd say, "I'm wanting a good reason, and what better than a fine big boy to these onions?"

And what like of a stew would it be but Irish?

Pause of respect before returning to the trough

Trinity College was referred to in passing. . . .

Well, there's all the usual cultural propaganda: Dates and Famous Names, impressive Corinthian entablatures and porticoes, balustrades and pediments and eighteenth-century atmosphere. . . .

(See pages 24 and 25 of the nearest Guide Book for the full chatter.)

. . . but, outside the Library, dignified, desolate, dehumanised, there are these *Two Seated Figures*. . . .

(Henry Moore—who else?)

. . . male and female, King and Queen, elementals, carved, sculpted, scraped, hewn, hollowed, moulded, cast in bronze, weathered, greening, smoothed, rounded, angular, pierced, passive, not so much faced as masked, more stone than metal, trapped in the present but long since older than the time around them, part of the landscape lost beneath these orderings of architecture, shapes from the legend, shadows from the dream, rooted elsewhere, distant drums, ancient battles, dark and obscure strivings, reverberations, mysteries, silence. . . .

The American with two Japanese cameras paused, checked how much film he had left in each . . . and obviously decided that it was about now he should grab a cuppa coffee someplace.

★　　★　　★

To make Irish Stew the way my grandmother would you need a thick iron pot about two feet across. . . .

"Will you be bringing me the bastable now?"

. . . with a flat lid to it, and a couple of lugs for hanging over the open fire if you've a need, and three stumps of legs for standing to the side of the hearth or in the oven.

And, for a table of plates to be filled the like of ours, you need a couple or three pounds of good fat neck of lamb, being the cheapest cut, a dozen or so fresh potatoes, three or four good big onions, and a sprig of young thyme. You leave the meat on the bone, just chopping it small as you've a mind to. Then you slice two or three of the potatoes, and line the bottom of the pot with them to cook away and thicken the juices you'll be getting. Then a layer of sliced onions, then the meat. A fist of rough salt, a scatter of pepper, then the thyme, and the rest of the onions, and then in with the whole potatoes. A good pint of water, cover the pot with the lid, and cook in the oven for a couple of hours till the smell of it has everybody waiting hungry. Or, if you like, you can simmer the pot on the stove. And, if you want carrots, cook a handful in a pan of water on their own, or the stewing will be their death.

("Facts that appear trivial," says Donald Davie, so he does, "are made important simply by being remembered with affection.")

Though you'll be blessed by Saint Anthony himself to be finding a stew the like of *that* in the Restaurants of Dublin today!

True, if you've the money there's no end of Fine Fayre for your table: Dublin Bay Prawns, Clarenbridge Oysters, Boyne Salmon,

Limerick Ham, Tara and Wexford Cheeses, Kerrygold Butter . . .
even a place serving *Crêpes Colleen* (*pancakes filled with scrumptious
Sea Food*), and (so help me!) *Salmon Anna Liffey* . . . but my
grandmother cooked for more than money.

Then there was Sunday evening in the frontroom after coming
back from Benediction, tea finished, and the fire lit, and the gramophone in its polished walnut cabinet, the sort you'd have to keep
winding, even in the middle of it playing . . . and these scratchy old
records like listening through the rain on the corrugated iron roof of
the jakes out in the yard, but never heard since with the same joy and
innocence, the same tears so unashamed, the same feelings of love
and tenderness and belonging. . . .
And wouldn't they be of our own Count John McCormack
himself?
With my grandmother and the little drop of something taken. . . .
    Come Back to Erin
    . . . and herself wiping away the few tears over our Uncle Bill and
our Uncle Martin away across the sea in America, gone these last
four years come next Easter. . . .

When you land from the Atlantic in New York, when you finally get through Customs and Immigration and out of the great sheds and on to Twelfth Avenue beneath the West Side Elevated Highway, the first cobble-stones you tread on are probably the same ones trodden by those Irish immigrants of the nineteenth and early twentieth century.

And I've still got this old snapshot of our Uncle Bill, probably in a drawer somewhere, haven't seen it in I don't know how long. . . .

Must look it out when I can get round to looking.

He's standing with a group of other young men on those cobbles, all in their best clothes—though what was "best" when you had to leave hearth and home for food to your stomach?

Can't remember if our Uncle Martin was with him . . . but they're all squinting up against the sun, all of them, the Hudson River in the background . . . hands for the building of America. . . .

Dead now, all of them, dead and buried. . . .

★   ★   ★

"Though what was there to be holding them *here*?" our Uncle Danny would say, with himself lost the left arm below the elbow during the Troubles or the First World War, and I too small to be knowing the difference then, "isn't it the God-forsaken bloody country?"

. . . and our mother giving him a look would curdle the milk at the words he was using, but not getting the farthing of change from *him*. . . .

"And they're writing every week nearly?" our Uncle Mike would say. . . .

"It's a fine letter Bill writes," my grandmother would say. "Which is a mercy on me in these last of my years."

. . . and our Uncle Mike would wink at our Uncle Danny, and our mother would find the one came Thursday, and read it out loud for my grandmother to hear again, with it about the land he'd journeyed to, where 'twas said the grass was greener, so it was, with the bread and work for all . . . and our Uncle Bart, whose name was really

73

Bartholomew, except that everybody called him Bart, or Young Bat as he was the youngest . . . and our Uncle Bart would smile to himself, so he would. . . .

"Doesn't that Detroit sound the grand city?" he'd say. . . .

"And if you think it's yourself to be going next," my grandmother would say, "it's another think you've got coming!"

And then our Uncle Bart would wind up the gramophone again, and we'd each be let choose one. . . .

> *The Bard of Armagh*
> *My Snowy Breasted Pearl*

. . . and I can hear mine to this day, the tune, the voice, the words . . . not really knowing very much of what it was about, at all, nothing about parting, about leaving home and place and land, nothing about any of the sorrows I have known since. . . .

> Kathleen Mavourneen, the grey dawn is breaking,
>   The horn of the hunter is heard on the hill,
>   The lark from her light wing
>   The bright dew is shaking:
>   Kathleen Mavourneen, what, slumb'ring still?
> O hast thou forgotten how soon we must sever?
> O hast thou forgotten this day we must part?
> It may be for years, it may be for ever:
>   O why art thou silent, the voice of my heart?
> It may be for years, and it may be for ever:
>   Then why art thou silent, Kathleen Mavourneen?
>
> Mavourneen! Mavourneen! my sad tears are falling,
>   To think that from Erin and thee I must part!
> It may be for years, and it may be for ever:
>   Then why art thou silent, the voice of my heart?
> It may be for years, and it may be for ever:
>   Then why art thou silent, Kathleen Mavourneen?

. . . but I'd break my heart over it, sobbing a different sort of tears than the ones our mother could get out of me, and our mother would be a bit embarrassed, and try to comfort me, except that I'd be going to my grandmother and burying my face in her lap of damp ashes and moth-balls and the something taken, and our mother couldn't be saying much for our Uncle Mike being there. . . .

And then, to be cheering me up and making a change, our Uncle Bart would play the piano, all the old tunes and songs . . . and everybody to know them would be joining in . . . and our Uncle Danny would sing *The Croppy Boy* or *Avenging and Bright are the Swift Swords of Erin*, so he would, with him sweating with the heat and the drink, and holding the box of matches under the stump of his left arm to be striking one for to light his pipe, and starting again when he had it going, with our Uncle Bart thumping away, and the glasses chinking on the top of the piano with it. . . .

> We are the Boys of Wexford,
>   Who fought with heart and hand,
>   To ease the pain
>   Of galling chain,
>   And free our Native Land!

. . . with the tiredness feathering down on us younger ones, fighting it and forcing our eyes to keep open, with them smarting from the smoke and the heat and the sleep coming, and our mother seeing the state of us, and sending us to bed, with only the look

needed to still the tongues of us . . . and our sister Anne taking us up, the passage and the stairs and the room cold, and the rim of the chamber-pot cold to our bums, and her quick fingers warm, and us hearing them all still singing and talking down there in the front-room, and the bed cold, but snuggling in after saying our Prayers, and her kissing us, with her face and breath warm . . . and the door closing, and lying in the darkness, whispering, and hearing it all going on down there. . . .

God Save Ireland! sing we proudly,
God Save Ireland! sing we all:
Whether on the scaffold high,
Or on the battle-field we die,
O what matter when for Erin dear we fall?

. . . the piano and the songs and the words and the voices, our Uncles, and our mother, and our father, and the others of us, and. . . .

Come, Child of Misfortune, hither,
I'll weep with thee tear for tear. . . .

. . . the sadness and the misery of it, and our grandmother, *my* grandmother with her . . . sons and daughters of. . . .
O Clement, O Loving, O Sweet. . . .
. . . until the feathers of, the wings of . . . sleep . . . came, and the . . . music drifted and became part of . . . all the rivering waters of . . . the long dream of. . . .

★   ★   ★

Well, *that's* a river to be running into more than the sea. . . .
Though even the Liffey tides out to meet her returning sons and homing daughters, past the docks and the restraining walls, the hundred cares and a tithe of troubles . . . in guilt and in glory . . . far calls. . . .

76

But it's all been done before, this description of Dublin as you approach by sea from Holyhead or Liverpool,

Once or twice, of several times, by men whom one cannot hope
To emulate. . . .

Simply pour a pint of plain into a gallon of foaming blarney, sprinkle on a thick fist of instant nostalgia, and whisk thoroughly until the mixture is light and creamy. Leave to that fermentation of the soul peculiar to the spirit of the place, and serve with liberal dollops of steaming sentimentality.

The Hill of Howth and the Bay, Dun Laoghaire and the Harbour. . . .

You glide on in the darkness, facing forward, the engines throbbing, other sons and daughters watching at the rail with you, many voices. . . .

"Will there be a train for Cork at this hour?"

"Didn't I send them the telegram from Manchester before leaving?"

"How long's it been since last time?"

Salt tasting on your lips . . . sea-mist . . . the bow-wave phosphorescent and cresting and surging past and back. . . .

Ground swell. . . .

And there are the lights of the distant city . . . other, smaller stars above it, others leading to it along Merrion Strand from Blackrock to Irishtown, looping and curving. . . .

"Wonder will they be there to meet us?"

"And why wouldn't they be?"

You glide closer out of the darkness, and the lights become windows and street-lamps and buses trundling along the coast road . . . there are the piers of the little harbour. . . .

"Won't be long now."

Though it always takes longer than it has any reason to, even with the train waiting, and the watchers patient, and everybody wanting to be off and away to wherever. . . .

"Will there be time for a drink?"

"And why wouldn't there be?"

77

Yes, there'll be time enough for most things. . . .
Leaving again, *and* returning.

I recently did return to Dublin with my wife and our children,
with it being their first time of going, and, faithful unto the last
letter of the tattered ould script, I traipsed them around some of the
places I hadn't seen for I don't know how many loving years . . . and,
eventually, after a couple of choking days and aching nights, when
I had the heart enough, and it thumping like Uncle Bart on that
piano in the frontroom, I walked them along the pavements and
across the roads and squares towards. . . .

Towards *what?*

Well, I know it must sound pretentious. . . .

*"Holy Mother of God!" says he, "isn't it back to your own Home
you were going? And it'll be a poor day when a Dublin man can't be
allowing a few words of emotion to be passing his lips at such a time,
surely!"*

. . . but it was some sort of journey into the interior of more than
a geographical location. . . .

"Ah!" says he, "didn't we have the latitude and longitude given?"
. . . more than a City, even Dublin. . . .

"The Metropolis as Metaphor," says Shem the Penman's Latest
Commentator, proffering yet another Skeleton Key or something. . . .

I only knew that this walking was through more than the evocative
names on some autobiographical street-map, more than the flipped
pages of some sentimental gazetteer of the soul . . . and that when we
at last reached wherever it was I was taking them, when I found what
I thought I was looking for, I wouldn't just read the script I had
rehearsed so often before this time and place, remember the pre-
pared words and gestures, put on the appropriate mask, assume the
proper voice . . . but I would stand back from the occasion, and
merely allow Dublin to speak with Dublin's own voice. . . .

"There," I would say, "there is the house in which I was born."
And we turned the corner from the Square. . . .
The whole block had been razed to the gound.
Redevelopment: *Proposed Offices for.* . . .
Dublin's own voice.

★　　★　　★

The face of this girl on the bus out along the Chapelizod Road. . . .
(Wonder whatever became of Teresa Riordan?)

Sixteen, seventeen, curly black hair, blue eyes, wide mouth, dimpled chin, the sort of complexion Nature did intend. . . .

But how to find words for the beauty of the world?

Youth, innocence, serenity, the Madonna of the Seven Dolours, perhaps Primavera about to dance off and litter the Fifteen Acres with roses or scatter lilies into the Liffey, the Flower of the Mountain, her breasts all perfume and her smile whispering Yes. . . .

She turned to her mate: "Will youse lend us a fag till tonight?"
(Still got that Sacred Heart Medal.)

79

All changed, voice, words, and script, *changed utterly:*

REMEMBER! *All* Visitors to Dublin!
When *You* are in *O'Connell Street*
(which may be fitly called *our* FIFTH AVENUE)
You can capture
and bring home
(at no extra charge!)
YOUR Glorious Memories of Ireland's *Enchantment!*

(Another thing to remember is that, in the scholarly opinion of *some*, if certain manifestations of Irish culture *can* inform us of the Irish people, "it will certainly not be to teach us their high degree of civilisation, nor their good taste, but rather to reveal to us a profound barbarism trying to imitate, as well as possible, more civilised neighbours."

"Well, now," says himself, *says he, "isn't that the fine scholar and gentleman to be talking! Mother of God!" says he, "weren't we the bloody Glory and Wonder of the Western World when the likes of him were running around skin-naked in blue bloody woad!"*

Though, again, there *are* others who murmur of "the most astonishing of human reveries, one of the most mysterious caprices of the intellect."

"Which," says himself, *"is nearer the bloody mark!")*

For, it says here in so many commercial words (chink, chink), Dublin is Erin's Shop Window, and *Genuine* Irish Souvenirs (avoid imitations!) include your actual Comical Stuffed Leprechauns, Endearing Connemara Dolls Dressed in Traditional Native Costume, Shamrock Ashtrays in various Indigenous Materials (as wood, stone, metal, and plastic), Model Turf Carts complete with Colourful Peasant and Quaint Donkey, Miniature Shillelaghs, the Glittering Loveliness of Waterford Cut Lead-Crystal Decanters and Table Suites in several different styles (as champagne, claret, sherry, port, liqueur, cocktail, quarter and half-pint tumblers, and goblets, with cutting based on Traditional Designs), Wood-Carving, Brassware, Antique Bric-a-Brac, Hand-Woven Wool and Tweed Scarves,

Stoles, Rugs, and Ties with Authentic Embroidered Family Crests, Exquisite Hand-Crafted Belleek China Renowned since 1957 (being Collector's Pieces of Highly Ornamented Jugs, Dishes, and Bowls, many in the Famous Lacy Openwork Pattern), Gramophone Records of Traditional Irish Folk Songs, Hand-Carved Saints and Sinners of Ancient Ireland, Amusing Wall-Plaques, Salad Bowls, Delicate Carrickmacross Lace Worked by the Nuns of County Monaghan in, er, Traditional Designs of Butterflies, Shamrocks, and Harps, Donegal and Aran Hand-Knitted Sweaters, Bawneen Fisherman's Pullovers and Cardigans (Products of Genuine Cottage Industries in the Homes of our People, where *bainin*, the Pure Undyed Wool from Mountain Sheep, Spun on the Ould Spinning-Wheel Famous in Song and Story, has been Woven on Hand-Looms for Centuries in the Romantic West of Ireland), and Irish Linen, Famous Everywhere for Beauty and Durability, Endless and Magical in Selection: Damask Tablecloths in Celtic and Floral Patterns, or Hand-Painted with Softly Muted Flower Sprays, with Supper, Tea, and Tray-Cloths, Hand-Embroidered in Donegal, and a Wide

Range of Bed-Linen, Hand-Painted Guest Towels, Napkin Sets
Embroidered with Scenes of Rural Life, Luncheon Sets in Superb
Contemporary or, er, Traditional Designs and Colours, Kitchen-
Cloths Printed with Amusing Incidents and Actual Events from
Irish History, Handkerchiefs with Personal Initials, Cocktail Sets,
Bolster Sets, and. . . .

But who *can* finish that sort of list?

Gifts and Purchases mailed, Duty Free, to all Countries.

Just so long as you remember that all prices ought to be quoted in
quids *and* dollars.

Footnote: If you really want that Pot of Gold at the End
of Finian's Rainbow, remember to bring home a Ticket in
the Irish Sweep! *On Sale Everywhere!*

Heard this one in a pub off Westmoreland Street:

It seems that when Almighty God had finished the making of
Ireland He was surprised to see a delegation waiting on Him from
all the other countries of the brand-new world.

"Well now," He said, "what else can I be doing for you?"

"Well," they said, politely enough, "we've been admiring Your
latest handiwork, and er—well, we were wondering just why You,
er, sold the rest of us so short?"

"What on earth do you mean?" He said, making the second joke
of all time.

"Well," they said after they'd finished laughing, "we admit that
the rest of the world has got its points, but it's perfectly obvious to
us that this Ireland is a little bit of Heaven You've let slip from out
the sky today, and it, er, doesn't seem quite fair on the likes of us
who've got to go on living in such places as the Garden of Eden."

"Ah!" said Almighty God, "but what *you* don't know is that
I'm leaving Old Nick to the making of the Irish."

82

A City, then, in (or so it says here) "spiritual, cultural, and moral disintegration," thick with the dust from the "collapse of traditional order and values" or something . . . "houses, lines of houses, streets, miles of pavements, piled-up bricks, stones," property belonging to landlords who never die . . . those "brick brown houses" which, according to James Joyce himself, are the "very incarnation of Irish paralysis."

Bricks made flesh and blood?

Well, it wasn't like *him* to be dropping a brick unless he was aiming for somebody's big fat toe!

Streets littered with the husks of rhetoric, where even the truth gets to sound like the scutterings of mice through the columns of yesterday's newspapers in "our dry cellar". . . .

"All Irishmen," says Frank O'Conner, your actual true Irish himself, neat, so he is, "when they are shy," says he, "instantly fling out into some sort of pose. They keep on talking," says he, keeping on talking, "instead of shutting up."

(Which makes them the shyest people on the face of the listening earth, so it does, with who else able to slip a word in sideways?)

. . . where characters perambulate, alive by merely being known for the parts they play, smudges of local colour in "death's dream kingdom". . . .

"The personal legend," says Patricia Hutchins, "is still important to Irish life . . . anecdotes, criticisms, quotations. . . ."

(For if Ireland is a piece of land entirely surrounded by footlights, then Dublin is the dead centre of the stage, with the production Grand Opera, the singers comedians, and the performance continuous.)

. . . the men like involuntary monks, theologians of the trivial, born into Dublin as though into a televised monastery where the Rule of the Order stipulates the Poverty of newly-acquired affluence, the Chastity of ignorance, the Obedience of Professional Rebels, an additional Vow of Perpetual Non-Silence, and the painstaking illumination of their days and nights with intricate lies and Hand-Tinted dreams. . . .

"The world's most brilliantly and completely thwarted city," says

83

this Horace Reynolds, "where talk is the National pastime," says he, "glory, and disease," so he does.

(Though your Dublin man handles his dead language with the same sort of sentimental reverence with which he touches any other corpse, strewing it with the dried flowers of pleasantry as though they were the very buds of Spring. Hear him for the first time, and you'll believe yourself in the presence of an unpublished Poet, so you will. . . .

"Surely," he'll say, with the patter glib to his lilting tongue, "I'm after liking the head on me glass of Guinness thick enough to be churning into best butter, so I am!"

. . . but hear him churn that rancid margarine for the tenth time or the twenty-first, cranking the same handle, using the same form of easy words, and you'll know that the words are cranking *him*, that he can no longer tell the difference between margarine and even imported butter.)

"It is a lovely city which arouses by affection," says the Anglican Bishop of Clogher, wherever *that* is, "but it is also an exasperating city which makes me feel frustrated," says he, "because the people of Dublin are not seriously interested in anything that happens outside Dublin."

(True, they watch the rioting in Belfast on the Television News, but isn't Belfast merely a suburb to the North of Glasnevin, surely?)

. . . the women abstaining from their own flesh, preserving it in white plaster to be cast by their celibate clergy into the moulds of the Ten Most Popular Saints on the Sacerdotal Hit Parade, "exploiting every emotion but their own," wept over by the stanza, sobbed about in song, the Wild Queens of the Western World whose lovely names have been echoed through the Marble Halls and bleary Saloons of umpteen Saturday night booze-ups . . . but whose nervous Kings prefer the barmaid, the biddable, the domestic. . . .

"The Rose of Tralee?" says this one of a pair of girls queuing up for *The Sound of Music* in a cinema on O'Connell Street. "The boys look at you here as though you've got the greenfly!"

And her friend laughed, both beautiful, each in their own way: "I'll tell you," says she, "compared to the boys in England the boys in Dublin are deadly. They make me feel as though I'm a freak, so they do."

(The best way for a Dubliner to see Dublin without benefit of either clergy or Tourist Board is to catch the boat for Holyhead and elsewhere.)

For George Bernard Shaw the place remained what it had been in 1870: a city of "foul-mouthed, foul-minded derision and obscenity," where "young men are still drivelling in slack-jawed blackguardism."

(Yet it was the same George Bernard Shaw who, in 1916, said that the executed Leaders of the Easter Rising would take their place in the political mythology of Ireland beside Robert Emmet and the Manchester Martyrs, and then went on: "I am bound to contradict any implication that I can regard as a traitor any Irishman

THEATRE · DAME STREET · DUBLIN · HANDCROFT? –

taken in a fight for Irish Independence against the British Government, which was a fair fight in everything except the enormous odds my countrymen had to face.")

For Brendan Behan Dublin was. . . .

But *that's* a list which, like the O'Connell Bridge, is a bloody sight broader than it's long, so it is!

For give your Dublin man the whistle of a tune one night, and he'll sing it to an early grave by the end of the week, so he will: meaning that few of them know when to stop anything. . . .

"And aren't you the fine Dublin man?" says himself. . . .

. . . a joke that has been flattened to boredom and back, a point that has been hammered home and out again through the kitchen window, an argument that has been elaborated and lost in the coruscating labyrinth of "interweaving and commingling" ornamentation. . . .

(Peace, Finnegan!)

. . . a fight in which even the bystanders start to get knocked down with a fist to the wrong gob . . . then the boot to the arse of a man who wasn't there a minute ago, a stone for a woman passing across the far side of the street . . . a petrol-bomb for anybody with the bad cess to be getting in the way of it . . . a bullet, a stick of gelignite, and what the bloody hell next?

"Glory be to God!" says himself. "When it's put like that the only bloody wonder is how we're let get away with it at all!"

Well, one possible explanation was offered by George Orwell, so it was, with him sticking the sharp pin into Sean O'Casey at the time. . . .

"Wouldn't that be the bold man now!"

"The basic reason," says he, "is probably England's bad conscience. It is difficult," says he, "to object to Irish Nationalism without seeming to condone centuries of English tyranny and exploitation. So," says he, "literary judgement is perverted by political sympathy. . . ."

"And isn't it time enough we were getting our natural rights?" says himself, "with sympathy cheaper than bloody justice?"

But let it go, let it tarry all the way to Tara and back—for who wants to be spitting on the graves of the Irish dead?

86

GARDINER STREET. DUBLIN
HASCRAFT

A last epiphany: A slum somewhere off Gardiner Street, between there and the Mater Misericordiae Hospital, with these two Doric pilasters, one either side of the open frontdoor, and an elegant fanlight over it, ribbed and arched, three curved petals of glass broken and repaired with bits of cardboard cut from a carton which had once held packets of Golden Wonder Potato Crisps, the lettering faded but readable. . . .

Bacon-flavoured

. . . the other four petals almost black with dirt in their rusting flounces of wrought-iron. . . .

The guitars and drums of Pop music throbbing from the darkness of the passage, on radio or record-player, Number One on the Charts. . . .

And this little girl squatting on the step, no shoes to her feet, and them filthy, this bottle of Pepsi-Cola held between the flesh of her thighs, almost empty, the end of the straw soggy . . . picking her nose in total self-absorption. . . .

"A day," might have said the Ginger Man, had he been coming along the pavement, "on which all things are born like uncovered stars."

And yet, and yet. . . .

The very lies of these pavements are truer than most gold-plated truisms, and good men have died for them.

Easter, 1916. . . .

In the name of God and of the dead generations from which she receives her old tradition of nationhood, Ireland, through us, summons her children to her flag. . . .

Thomas Clarke, Sean MacDiarmada, Patrick Pearse, MacDonagh, Kent, Joe Plunkett, James Connolly. . . .

"Listen," our Uncle Mike would say, "just one hour before the British shot Joe Plunkett in the stone-breaking yard of Kilmainham Jail, which was at the first light of the dawn on the fourth day of the month of May in the year of the Easter Rising, nineteen-hundred-and-sixteen, so it was, they let him marry with Grace Gifford. Had her to wait in the Chapel, led Joe in, and him handcuffed with the gall of iron, and these twenty brave British soldiers with their loaded guns and bayonets of steel for the fear of the one man, and they let him be married by a Priest of the Church with poor Grace Gifford, and her weeping since the sentence was passed. Not one minute was she given alone with her man, but the brave soldiers there watching. Till they took him from her, and him never out of the galling of the iron, and marched him to the wall of the stone-breaking yard, and shot him down with their guns like the bloody murderers they are! Now wouldn't the like of that be breaking a heart of stone itself?"

"Tell us about James Connolly," we'd say. . . .

And our Uncle Mike would take down the book from the shelf, and turn to the page, with it opening easy there from having been opened so many times before, and read us the words. . . .

"What you'll just have to be remembering," he'd say when he had the place, as though we could ever forget, "was that James Connolly was a wounded man, him with the bones of his leg shattered already by the bullet of a British gun, with them jabbing out of his flesh to his mortal agony, and they had him lying with his wounds in Dublin Castle, guarded, unable to stir neither foor nor hand of him. . . . And this is the Signed, Sworn, and Witnessed Account of his last minutes on this soil, written by the Priest of the Church who administered the

89

Last Rites to him on that day, the twelfth of the month of May, so it was, with the Priest being Father Aloysius. . . ."

They carried him from his bed in an ambulance stretcher, down to a waiting ambulance and drove him to Kilmainham Jail. They carried him from the ambulance to the Jail yard and put him in a chair. . . . He was very brave and cool. . . . I said to him, "Will you pray for the men who are about to shoot you?" and he said: "I will say a prayer for all brave men who do their duty." His prayer was: "Forgive them for they know not what they do." And then they shot him. . . .

And our Uncle Mike, a fine big man, would be reading with the tears running down his cheeks. . . .

At four o'clock, when the shooting was done, a gentle rain began to fall—the tears of Dark Rosaleen. . . .

And I wept with our Uncle Mike then, and I have wept since. . . .

So there it is: a city of laughter in which it is so easy to weep, a place of prayer so close to being a den of thieves. . . .

"Jesus, Mary, and Joseph!" says he, "aren't you the great one with an insult? So it's thieves we are, is it?"

90

In the sense that we desecrate our own Temple, deny our own Power, doubt our own Glory, steal from our Past to mortgage our Future, suffer the loss of our Souls for the price of a Guinness—yes, we are.

"Well now," says he, eyeing the last knockings in the bottom of his fourth or seventh pint of plain, it being the only drink for a man. . . .

With Guinness standing for more than Guinness, being more than the celebrated National Beverage . . . for wasn't there another occasion when a son sold his birthright for a dish of stew to his stomach and a quick sup of drink to his thirst?

A place of prayer, then, where blasphemy is so easy on the lips, stale language the like of this blathering so thoughtless on the tongue, the part in the play simpler to act than the life is to live.

"Would you be taking another?" says he, with his glass in his fist. . . .

And there are the two ways of walking through this city of the mind:

You can start at page one of the Guide Book, spread the map wide, find out where you're at now, check the reference, decide where you want to go (which will be where everybody else will be going sooner or later), what you want to see first (which will be what many others will be seeing), make a list of all the Historic Streets and

91

Houses, Ancient Cathedrals and Churches, Libraries, Art Galleries, Notable Public Buildings (not forgetting the General Post Office and the National Museum), Parks and Gardens and the Elegant Georgian Squares. . . .

Fitzwilliam, Parnell (formerly known as Rutland), Merrion. . . .

"Wasn't Merrion Square bought by the Church for to build a cathedral?" said another citizen who hadn't opened his mouth yet. "But the ground was a bog to the knees, so it would have sunk like the Titanic. Which would be as good an end for a cathedral as you'd want—for what do we need a new House of God when we've the desperate shortage of decent houses for the people? Though there's talk the new Archbishop will be opening Merrion to the public as a garden any day now, with it private to the use of the Nuns, which isn't before time."

Or you can walk the way it comes. . . .

Taking the route you would be likely to take
From the place you would be likely to come from. . . .

(Has no American scholar been able to demonstrate the descent of Thomas Stearns Eliot from Irish stock?)

Stopping to listen to the citizens. . . .

. . . starting from anywhere,
And any time or at any season. . . .

(Except, of course, the Season of the Summer Tourist.)

. . . even when the citizens want to be pursuing their own subjects, which may not always be *your* subjects, but which all have a part in the pattern of the City, even though you do not at first see what possible pattern there can be. . . .

For *this* "is to circumspect," to go by way of whatever takes your fancy at the time of starting, to try this pub or that church, to cross the street or be dandering around the nearest corner, over the Liffey on the South Circular Road and back by Butt Bridge into Tara Street with all the sights and sounds and songs and swearing between, all the faces and places and shop-windows and mornings and evenings and remembrance of things past and thoughts of. . . .

"Now wouldn't that be the walk of all the world, surely," says he. . . .

And it's all there still: the past, the present, the dead centre and the expanding circumference, the dry root and the green tree, old stone to new building, the City as Metaphor, the National Museum on Kildare Street and Bingo in the most unlikely places, Heaven a few streets north of Donnybrook, Hell to the south of Drumcondra, Purgatory this side of the Guinness Brewery, Limbo between there and Clontarf. . . .

(*I had not thought death had undone so many.*)

The "timidity and the hollowness of its gestures . . . charming apathy and shiftlessness . . . solemnisation without solemnity."

(Thank *you*, Anthony Burgess.)

Words, songs, tunes, sights, sounds, tastes, memories of the way it used to be, the drift of change, fears of what it will probably become if it hasn't already, hopes that the good will get better, that the best is yet to be, that. . . .

But the little girl squatting on the step somewhere off Gardiner Street . . . it is *her* Dublin, no longer mine.

I wonder does her grandmother ever. . . .

(Now where did I leave that sixth colour-slide?)

And how can you possibly stop in the middle of a. . . .

BACHELOR'S WALK. DUBLIN [signature]